CONTENTS

D0469712

INTRODUCTION

The SAY IT RIGHT FOREIGN LANGUAGE PHRASE BOOK SERIES has been developed with the conviction that learning to speak a foreign language should be fun and easy!

All SAY IT RIGHT phrase books feature the EPLS Vowel Symbol System, a revolutionary phonetic system that stresses consistency, clarity, and above all, simplicity!

Since this unique phonetic system is used in all SAY IT RIGHT phrase books, you only have to learn the EPLS VOWEL SYMBOL SYSTEM ONCE!

The SAY IT RIGHT series uses the easiest phrases possible for English speakers to pronounce and is designed to reflect how foreign languages are used by native speakers.

You will be amazed at how confidence in your pronunciation leads to an eagerness to talk to other people in their own language.

Whether you want to learn a new language for travel, education, business, study, or personal enrichment, SAY IT RIGHT phrase books offer a simple and effective method of pronunciation and communication.

PRONUNCIATION GUIDE

Most English speakers are familiar with the word **Korea.** This is how the correct pronunciation is represented in the EPLS Vowel Symbol System.

All Korean vowel sounds are assigned a specific non-changing symbol. When these symbols are used in conjunction with consonants and read normally, pronunciation of even the most difficult foreign word becomes incredibly EASY!

On the following page are all the EPLS Vowel Symbols used in this book. They are EASY to LEARN since their sounds are familiar. Beneath each symbol are three English words which contain the sound of the symbol.

Practice pronouncing the words under each symbol until you mentally associate the correct vowel sound with the correct symbol. Most symbols are pronounced the way they look!

THE SAME BASIC SYMBOLS ARE USED IN ALL SAY IT RIGHT PHRASE BOOKS!

EPLS VOWEL SYMBOL SYSTEM

Ⓐ
Ace
Bake
Safe

ⒺⒺ
See
Feet
Meet

Ⓞ
Oak
Cold
Sold

⑳
Cool
Pool
Too

ⓔ
Men
Red
Bed

ⓐⓗ
Hot
Dot
Mop

ⓐ
Cat
Sad
Had

ⓤⓗ
Up
Sun
Cup

ⓘ
Win
Sit
Give

ⓞⓤ
Would
Should
Could

ⒺⒺ This EPLS Vowel Symbol has been narrowed to indicate visually that this sound is barely pronounced. On the next page we will explain its importance.

EPLS VOWEL SYMBOL ENHANCEMENTS

On the previous page are all the EPLS Vowel Symbols used in this book. They are EASY to LEARN since most of their sounds are familiar.

EPLS has enhanced the following vowel symbols below by narrowing them in order to visually help you recognize that their respective sounds are shortened.

When narrow vowel symbols appear together (example below), it reminds you to blend their respective sounds evenly like the **eo** in **Leo** or **leo**tard.

EXAMPLE: The Korean word for "chair" is:

Additionally, when a narrow vowel symbol appears by itself, you likewise shorten its sound.

Remember, the best way to perfect your Korean pronunciation is to listen to a Native Speaker. This is important because there are a couple of sounds which have no English equivalent.

EPLS CONSONANTS

Consonants are letters like **T**, **D**, and **K**. They are easy to recognize and their pronunciation seldom changes. However, in Korean, the pronunciation of a particular letter will be affected by the letters in front of it or directly following.

The following pronunciation guide letters represent EPLS representations of Hangul consonants.

B Pronounce this **EPLS** letter like the rolled Spanish **r**.

G Pronounced like the **g** in **g**eese.

J Pronounced like the **j** in **j**eep.

Y Pronounced like **ye** in **ye**s.

CH Pronounce these letters like **ch** in **ch**air

GW Pronounce these **EPLS** letters like **gu** in La**Gu**ardia Airport or the **gu** in i**gu**ana.

HW This unique paring of consonants is the reverse of the English **wh** in **wh**at. The **EPLS HW** sound is an aspirated "H" made by breathing out as you might do when making a sigh of relief, and at the same time pronouncing the **HW**. Practice pronouncing the English word **wh**ey.

DD **Double Consonants** are pronounced like their corresponding counterparts, but more quickly and boldly.

THE HANGUL ALPHABET

Hangul Vowels

아, 야, 어, 여, 오, 요, 우, 유, 으, 이

Hangul Consonants

ㄱ, ㄴ, ㄷ, ㄹ, ㅁ, ㅂ, ㅅ, ㅇ, ㅈ, ㅊ,
ㅋ, ㅌ, ㅍ, ㅎ

The Hangul alphabet has 10 vowels and 14 consonants. However, because of combination vowels and double consonants, the end result is over 40 characters. Add to that number the pronunciation changes that occur based on where a particular vowel or consonant is located in the word - beginning, middle, or end - then the alphabet increases dramatically.

Hangul Characters

~   This character precedes a Korean word or phrase and indicates that there is a word spoken before. You will usually see this in phrasemakers.

(은/는)   You will see characters in parentheses, especially in phrasemakers or at the beginning of sentences. EPLS has shown these characters as Korean Native Speakers might say them; however, they are not transliterated in the EPLS and do not affect the grammar or understanding of the spoken word.

PRONUNCIATION TIPS

- Each pronunciation guide word is broken into syllables. Read each word slowly, one syllable at a time, increasing speed as you become more familiar with the system.

- In the Korean language all syllables are spoken with the same pitch. No syllable is stressed and the meaning of a word is not dependent on stress or pitch.

- When asking a question in Korean, use a rising pitch on ending the sentence or word to indicate a **question**.

- Articles like **a**, **an** or **the** are not a part of the Korean language. In the Korean language a reference to something is determined by context.

- Korean is either polite, formal, or informal. In this book, EPLS has chosen in most cases to use words and phrases that are polite.

- To perfect your Korean accent you must listen closely to Korean speakers and adjust your speech accordingly.

- Korean people love to have foreigners make an effort to speak their language, and many Koreans speak some English, as they are taught English early in their schooling.

- The pronunciation choices in this book were chosen for their simplicity and effectiveness.

ICONS USED IN THIS BOOK

KEY WORDS

You will find this icon at the beginning of chapters indicating key words relating to chapter content. These are important words to become familiar with.

PHRASEMAKER

The Phrasemaker icon provides the traveler with a choice of phrases that allows the user to make his or her own sentences.

Say It Right in
KOREAN

ESSENTIAL WORDS AND PHRASES

Here are some basic words and phrases that will help you express your needs and feelings in **Korean**. Note that there is one basic greeting and one standard response that is used in most situations. This greeting can be polite or informal.

Hello / How are you? / Good morning / Good afternoon / Good evening

Hello

안녕하세요

ⓐN-NYⓤNG Hⓐ-Sⓔ-Yⓞ

Yes, hello (Reply)

네, 안녕하세요

Nⓔ ⓐN-NYⓤNG Hⓐ-Sⓔ-Yⓞ

Hello (Informal)

안녕

ⓐN-NYⓤNG

Hello (Informal reply)

안녕

ⓐN-NYⓤNG

Good night (Polite)

안녕히 주무세요

ⓐⓗN-NYⓤⓗNG-H㉒
Jⓞⓞ-Mⓞⓞ-S㉒-Yⓞ

See you later.

나중에 만나요

Nⓐⓗ-JⓞⓞNG-㉒   MⓐⓗN-Nⓐⓗ-Yⓞ

Good-bye (Said to the person leaving.)

안녕히 가세요

ⓐⓗ-NYⓤⓗNG-H㉒   Gⓐⓗ-S㉒-Yⓞ

Good-bye (Said to the person staying as you leave.)

안녕히 계세요

ⓐⓗ-NYⓤⓗNG-H㉒   G㉒-S㉒-Yⓞ

Bye (Informal)

안녕

ⓐⓗN-NYⓤⓗNG

Note: Polite and informal: In Korean, things can be said in a polite or informal way. As a visitor, it is best to err on the polite side in most cases. Sometimes, especially with children, polite may be too polite, but you will be understood. In this book, phrases will be polite unless indicated as informal.

Yes

네 / 예

N(ẽ) / Y(ẽ)

No

아니요

(ah)-N(EE)-Y(O)

Thank you

감사합니다

K(ah)M-S(ah)-H(ah)M-N(EE)-D(ah)

Excuse me

실례합니다

SH(O)L-L(ẽ)-H(ah)M-N(EE)-D(ah)

I'm sorry

죄송합니다

CH(ẽ)-S(O)NG-H(ah)M-N(EE)-D(ah)

Note: The word **"Please"** does not exist by itself in Korean. The word "please" in polite speech is automatically implied. On the next page you will see the phrase "Please repeat". "Please" is represented by S(ẽ)-Y(O) in the EPLS transliteration.

I don't understand!

이해가 안되요!

ⒺⒺ-Hⓐ-Gⓐⓗ ⓐⓗN-DWⓔ-Yⓞ

Do you understand?

이해가 되십니까?

ⒺⒺ-Hⓔ Gⓐⓗ-TWⓔ-SHⓘM-NⒺⒺ-Gⓐⓗ

I'm a tourist.

저는 관광객 입니다.

Jⓤⓗ-NⓞⓤN GⓐⓗN-GⓐⓗNG-Gⓐ
GⓘM-LⒺⒺ-Dⓐⓗ

I don't understand Korean.

저는 한국말 못해요.

Jⓤⓗ-NⓞⓤN HⓐⓗN-GⓞⓞK-MⓐⓗL
Mⓞ-Tⓐ-Yⓞ

Do you speak English?

영어를 할줄 아세요?

YⓤⓗNG-ⓤⓗ-RⓞⓤL HⓐⓗL-JⓞⓞL ⓐⓗ-Sⓔ-Yⓞ

Please repeat.

다시 한번 말해주세요.

Dⓐⓗ-SHⒺⒺ HⓐⓗN-BⓤⓗN
MⓐⓗL-Hⓐ Jⓞⓞ-Sⓔ-Yⓞ

FEELINGS

Give me... (Polite)

~주세요.

...J⓪⓪-S(ⓔ)-Y⓪

I want...

~원해요.

...W(uh)N-H(A)-Y⓪

I have...

~가지고 있어요.

...G(ah)-J(EE)-G⓪ (EE)-S(uh)-Y⓪

I know.	**I don't know.**
~알아요.	~몰라요.
...(ah)-R(ah)-Y⓪	...M⓪L-L(ah)-Y⓪

I like...

~좋아해요.

...J⓪-(ah)-H(A)-Y⓪

I don't like...

~싫어해요.

...SH(i)-R(uh)-H(A)-Y⓪

~ Remember that this character precedes a
  Korean word or phrase and indicates that
  there is a word spoken before.

I'm lost.

저는 길을 잃었어요.

J⒰-N⒪N G⒠-R⒪L ⒠-R⒰-S⒰-Y⒪

We are lost.

우리는 길을 잃었어요.

⒬-R⒠-N⒪N G⒠-R⒪L
⒠-R⒰-S⒰-Y⒪

I'm ill.

저는 아파요.

J⒰-N⒪N ⒜-P⒜-Y⒪

I'm thirsty.

저는 목이 말라요.

J⒰-N⒪N M⒪-G⒠
M⒜L-L⒜-Y⒪

I'm hungry.

저는 배가 고파요.

J⒰-N⒪N B⒜̃-G⒜
G⒪-P⒜-Y⒪

I'm happy.

저는 행복해요.

J⒰-N⒪N H⒜̃NG-B⒪K-H⒜̃-Y⒪

INTRODUCTIONS

Use the following phrases when meeting someone for the first time both privately or in business.

My name is...

제 이름은... 입니다.

Jĕ EE-Rou-Moun...First and Last Name...
iM-NEE-Dah

What's your name?

이름(성함)이 무엇입니까?

EE-Duhm-EE (Suhng-Hah M-EE)
Moo-uh-SHiM-NEE-GGah

Very nice to meet you.

만나서 반가워요.

Mah N-Nah-Suh
Bah N-Gah-Wuh-YO

GENERAL GUIDELINES

Korea is a peninsula bordered to the west by China and to the east by Japan. South Korea is just under 100,000 square miles, and much of that area is made up of hills and mountains. Seoul is the capital. Although Korea is quite modern, it retains its identity through a keen respect for tradition and a reverence for its rich past and culture rooted on Confucian principals.

- Respect for elders and their place in society is of utmost importance.

- When you are trying to signal someone, place your palm down with fingers touching and move your hand up and down ever so slightly. It is considered impolite to gesture to someone with palms up.

- Hand shaking is a common practice, both on arrival and when taking leave.

- Taekwondo is the ultimate martial art discipline of Korea and is recognized in the Olympic Games.

- Seafood is a mainstay of Korean life because of Korea's location and access to great fishing in the Yellow Sea and the Sea of Japan.

THE BIG QUESTIONS

Who?

누구?

N⓪⓪-G⓪⓪

Who is it?

누구세요?

N⓪⓪-G⓪⓪-SⒶ-Y⓪

What?

뭐라고요?

Mⓤⓗ-Ⓡ⒜ⓗ-G⓪-Y⓪

What's that?

저것은 무엇입니까?

Jⓤⓗ-Gⓤⓗ-S⓪ⓤN

M⓪⓪-ⓤⓗ-SHⓘM-N⒠⒠-GG⒜ⓗ

When?

~언제요?

...ⓤⓗN-Jⓔ̌-Y⓪

Where?

~어디에서요?

...ⓤⓗ-D⒠⒠-ⓔ̌-Sⓤⓗ-Y⓪

Where is...?

~어디에 있나요?

...ⓤⓗ-ⓉⒺⒺ-ⓔ̆-ⓘN-Nⓐⓗ-Yⓞ

Which?

어떤거요?

ⓤⓗN-DDⓤⓗN-Gⓤⓗ-Yⓞ

Why?

왜요?

Wⓐ̂-Yⓞ

How?

어떻게요?

ⓤⓗ-Dⓤⓗ-Kⓐ-Yⓞ

How much? (money)

얼마인가요?

ⓤⓗL-Mⓐⓗ-ⓘN-Gⓐⓗ-Yⓞ

How long? (time)

얼마나 걸리나요?

ⓤⓗL-Mⓐⓗ-Nⓐⓗ
GⓤⓗL-LⒺⒺ-Nⓐⓗ-Yⓞ

ASKING FOR THINGS

The following phrases are valuable for directions, food, help, etc.

...give me. (Polite)

~주세요.

...J⓪⓪-S(ě)-Y⓪

...I need.

~필요해요.

...P(ĭ)-BY⓪-H(ě)-Y⓪

...can you?

~ 해줄수 있나요?

...H(ǎ)-J⓪⓪L-S⓪⓪ (ĭ)N-N(ǎ)-Y⓪

When asking a question it is polite to say "**May I ask**" and "**Thank you**".

May I ask?	**Thank you**
문의해도 될까요?	감사합니다
M⓪⓪-N(EE)-H(ǎ)-D⓪	G(ǎ)M-S(ǎ)-
DW(ě)-GG(ǎ)-Y⓪	H(ǎ)M-N(EE)-D(ǎ)

PHRASEMAKER

In English, we say **I would like coffee**. Question structure in Korean normally states the subject first, object second and verb last. For example, **"I, coffee, want"** shown below.

▶ **Coffee...**

커피

(K⑩-P㋐)

▶ **Water...**

물

(M㋡L)

▶ **Ice...**

얼음

(⑩-Ŗ㋡M)

▶ **The menu...**

메뉴

(M㋓-NY㋡)

I...want.

저는 ~ 원해요.

J⑩-N㋡N (K⑩-P㋐) W⑩N-H㋐-Y⓪

Note: Closed parentheses in the EPLS transliteration indicates where the object is inserted.

PHRASEMAKER

Here are a few sentences you can use when you feel the urge to say **I need**... or **can you**...?
Say what you need and then go to the bottom of the page and say ...PⓘL-RYⓄ-Hⓔ-YⓄ.

▶ **Your help...**

도움이...

DⓄ-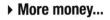M...

▶ **More money...**

돈이 더...

DⓄ-NⒺⒺ D...

▶ **Change...** (money)

잔돈(이)...

Jⓐ ⓗ N-DDⓄN...

▶ **A doctor...**   ▶ **A lawyer...**

의사...   변호사...

ⓞⓤⒺⒺ-Sⓐⓗ...   BYⓤⓗN-HⓄ-Sⓐⓗ...

...I need

~필요해요

...PⓘL-RYⓄ-Hⓔ-YⓄ

PHRASEMAKER

Say what you need and then
go to the bottom of the page and
say ...ⓘN-Nⓐh-Yⓞ.

▸ **Help me...**

도와줄수...

DⓄ-Wⓐh-JⓞⓞL-Sⓞⓞ...

▸ **Give me...**

줄수...

JⓞⓞL-Sⓞⓞ...

▸ **Tell me...**

말해줄수...

Mⓐh-Hⓐ̃-JⓞⓞL-Sⓞⓞ...

▸ **Take me to...**

데려가 줄수...

Dⓔ̃-RYⓤh-Gⓐh   JⓞⓞL-Sⓞⓞ...

...can you?

~있나요?

...ⓘN-Nⓐh-Yⓞ

ASKING THE WAY

No matter how independent you are, sooner or later you'll probably have to ask for directions.

Where is…?

~어디에 있나요?

...ⓤ-DⒺⒺ-ⓔ ⓘN-Nⓐⓗ-Yⓞ

I'm looking for…

~(을/를) 찾고 있어요.

...JⓐⓗT-Gⓞ ⒺⒺ-SSⓐⓗ-Yⓞ

Is it near?

가깝나요?

Gⓐⓗ-GGⓐⓗM-Nⓐⓗ-Yⓞ

Is it far?

먼가요?

MⓤⓗN Gⓐⓗ-Yⓞ

Left	**Right**
왼쪽	오른쪽
WⓔN-JJⓞK	ⓞ-BⓞⓤN-JJⓞK

PHRASEMAKER

Say what you need then go to the bottom of the page and say
...ⓐ-Dⓔⓔ-ⓔ ⓘN-Nⓐ-Yⓞ.

▶ **The restroom...**

화장실(은)...

HWⓐ-JⓐNG-SHⓘLN...

▶ **The telephone...**

전화기(는)...

Jⓤ)N-HWⓐ-GⓔⓔN...

▶ **The beach...**

바닷가(는)...

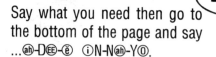

Bⓐ-Dⓐ)T-Gⓐ...

▶ **The hotel...**

호텔(은)...

HⓄ-Tⓔ)L-ⓞⓤN...

...where is?

~어디에 있나요?

...ⓐ-Dⓔⓔ-ⓔ ⓘN-Nⓐ-Yⓞ

TIME

What time is it?

몇시인가요?

MY⒰-SH㋎-㋑N-G⒜-Y⒪

Morning

아침

⒜-CH㋑M

Noon

점심

J⒰M-SH㋑M

Night

저녁

J⒰-NY⒰K

Today

오늘

㋩-N⒪L

Tomorrow

내일

N⒜-㋑L

This week

이번주

EE-BuhN-Joo

This month

이번달

EE-BuhN-DDahL

This year

이번 해 / 금년

e-BuhN-He / GouM-NYuhN

Now

지금

JEE-GouM

Soon

곧

GoT

Later

나중에

Nah-JooNG-e

Never

절대로

JuhL-DDae-Ro

WHO IS IT?

I (To a superior)
저
J(uh)

I (To an equal)
나
N(ah)

You (Polite or elder)   (To a younger person or friend)

당신   너

D(ah)NG-SH(i)N   N(uh)

He / She / It

그남자 / 그녀 / 그것

G(ou)-N(ah)M-J(ah) / G(ou)-NY(uh) / G(ou)-G(uh)T

You (Plural)

당신들 너희들

D(ah)NG-SH(i)N-D(ou)L N(uh)-H(EE)-D(uh)L

We

우리

(oo)-R̥(EE)

They

그들

G(ou)-D(ou)L

THIS AND THAT

The equivalents of **this, that, these** are as follows:

This

이것

EE-Guh T

This is mine.

이것은 제 것이예요.

EE-Guh-SouN Je-Guh-SHEE-Ye-Yo

That

저것

Juh-Guh T

That is mine.

저것은 제 것이예요.

Juh-Guh-SouN Je Guh-SHEE-Ye-Yo

These

이것들

EE-Guh T-DouL

These are mine.

이것들은 제 것 이예요.

EE-Guh T-Dou-RouN Je Guh-SHEE-Ye-Yo

USEFUL OPPOSITES

Near	**Far**
가까워요	멀어요
G@h-GG@h-W@h-Y⓪	M@h-R@h-Y⓪
Here	**There**
여기요	저기요
Y@h-G㋐-Y⓪	J@h-G㋐-Y⓪
Left	**Right**
왼쪽	오른쪽
W㋓N-JJ⓪K	⓪-R@w N-JJ⓪K
A little	**A lot**
조금요	많이요
J⓪-K@w M-Y⓪	M@h-N㋐-Y⓪
More	**Less**
더요	적어요
D@h-Y⓪	J@h-G@h-Y⓪
Big	**Small**
커요	작아요
K@h-Y⓪	J@h-G@h-Y⓪

Open	**Closed**
열어요	닫혔어요
Y⓪-Rⓤ-Y⓪	D⓪-CHYⓤ-SSⓤ-Y⓪

Cheap	**Expensive**
싸요	비싸요
SS⓪-Y⓪	Bⓔ-SS⓪-Y⓪

Dirty	**Clean**
더러워요	깨끗해요
Dⓤ-Rⓤ-Wⓤ-Y⓪	GGⓔ-GG⓸-T⓪-Y⓪

Good	**Bad**
좋아요	나빠요
J⓪-⓪-Y⓪	N⓪-BBⓤ-Y⓪

Vacant	**Occupied**
비어있어요	차있어요
Bⓔ-ⓤⓔ-SSⓤ-Y⓪	CH⓪-ⓔ-SSⓤ-Y⓪

Right	**Wrong**
맞아요	틀려요
M⓪-J⓪-Y⓪	T⓸L-LYⓤ-Y⓪

WORDS OF ENDEARMENT

I like you.

나는 당신을 좋아해요.

D@NG-SH①-⓪L N@-N⓪N
J⓪-@-H@-Y⓪

I love you.

나는 당신을 사랑해요.

N⑬-G@ D@NG-SH①-⓪L
S@-R@NG-H@-Y⓪

I like Korea.

저는 한국을 좋아해요.

Jⓤ-N⓪N H@N-G⓪⓪-G⓪L
J⓪-@-H@-Y⓪

I like Seoul.

저는 서울을 좋아해요.

Jⓤ-N⓪N Sⓤ-⓪⓪-R⓪L J⓪-@-H@-Y⓪

Kiss me!

키스 해주세요!

K㋓-S⓪ H⑬-J⓪⓪-S⑬-Y⓪

WORDS OF ANGER

What do you want?

용권이 뭡니까?

Y⓪NG-GWⓤN-㋞
MⓤM-N㋞-GGⓐ

Leave me alone!

저를 좀 나두세요!

Jⓤ-Ⓡ⓪L J⓪M
Nⓤ-D⓪-S㋞-Y⓪

Go away!

저리가요!

Jⓤ-Ⓡ㋞-Gⓐ-Y⓪

Be quiet!

조용히 해줘요!

J⓪-Y⓪NG-H㋞ Hⓐ-Jⓤ-Y⓪

That's enough!

이제 충분해요!

㋞-J㋞ CH⓪NG-B⓪N-Hⓐ-Y⓪

COMMON EXPRESSIONS

When you are at a loss for words but have the feeling that you should say something, try one of these!

No problem.

문제 없어요.

M⊚⊚N-J⊕̆   ⊕hP-S⊕h-Y⊚

Congratulations!

축하해요!

CH⊚⊚-K⊕h-H⊕̃-Y⊚

Good fortune!

복을 빌께요!

B⊚-G⊚ᵘL   B⊙L-GG⊕̆-Y⊚

Good luck!

행운을 빌께요!

H⊕̃NG-⊚⊚-N⊚ᵘL   B⊙L-GG⊕̆-Y⊚

Welcome!

어서 오세요!

⊕h-S⊕h   ⊚-S⊕̃-Y⊚

My goodness!

어머나!

uh-Muh-Nah

How beautiful!

너무 아름답네요!

Nuh-Mou ah-Roum-Dahm-Nĕ-YO

Of course!

당연하지요!

DahNG-Yuhn-Hah-JEE-YO

What a shame!

정말 부끄럽네요!

Juhng-Mahl
Boo-GGou-Ruhm-Nĕ-YO

Bravo!

브라보!

Bou-Rah-BO

Cheers!

환호!

HWahn-HO

USEFUL COMMANDS

Stop!

멈춰 주세요!

M⓪M-CH⓪ J⓪⓪-Sⓔ̃-Y⓪

Go!

가주세요!

Gⓐ J⓪⓪-Sⓔ̃-Y⓪

Wait!

기다려 주세요!

Gⓔⓔ-Dⓐ-RY⓪ J⓪⓪-Sⓔ̃-Y⓪

Hurry!

서둘러 주세요!

S⓪-D⓪⓪L-L⓪ J⓪⓪-Sⓔ̃-Y⓪

Slow down!

천천히 해주세요!

CH⓪N-CH⓪N-Hⓔⓔ Hⓐ̃-J⓪⓪-Sⓔ̃-Y⓪

Come here!

여기로 와주세요!

Y⓪-Gⓔⓔ-R⓪ Wⓐ-J⓪⓪-Sⓔ̃-Y⓪

EMERGENCIES

Fire!

불이야!

B⓪⓪-Ⓡ🅔🅔-Y🅐🅗

Help!

도와주세요!

D⓪-W🅐🅗-J⓪⓪-S🅔-Y⓪

Emergency!

긴급상황이예요!

K🅘N-G⓪⓪P-S🅐🅗NG-HW🅐🅗NG-🅔🅔-Y🅔-Y⓪

Call the police!

경찰을 불러 주세요!

GY🅤🅗NG-CH🅐🅗-Ⓡ⓪⓪L

B⓪⓪L-L🅤🅗   J⓪⓪-S🅔-Y⓪

Call an ambulance!

구급차를 불러 주세요!

G⓪⓪-G⓪⓪P-CH🅐🅗-Ⓡ⓪⓪L

B⓪⓪L-L🅤🅗   J⓪⓪-S🅔-Y⓪

ARRIVAL

Passing through customs should be easy since there are usually agents available who speak English. You may be asked how long you intend to stay and if you have anything to declare.

- Have your passport ready.

- Be sure all documents are up-to-date.

- You will be required to fill out a customs form declaring personal items that you are bringing into the country. It is very important to hold on to this form and to present it when leaving Korea.

- It is important to note that if you do not declare items on entry, you may be charged tax on these items on your departure.

- There is a set departure tax when leaving Korea.

- If you have connecting flights, be sure to reconfirm in advance and arrive 2 to 3 hours early for flights and lengthy customs processing.

- Make sure your luggage is clearly marked inside and out, and always keep an eye on it when in public places.

KEY WORDS

Baggage
수화물
S⑳-HW⑨-M⑩L

My baggage
제 수화물
J⑬-S⑳-HW⑨-M⑩L

Documents
서류
S⑪-RY⑳

Passport
여권
Y⑪-GW⑪N

Porter
짐을 옮길사람
J①-M⑪L-⑩LM-G①L-S⑨-R⑨M

Taxi
택시
T⑨K-SH⑯

USEFUL PHRASES

Here is my passport.

제 여권은 여기에 있어요.

Jⓔ Y⓾-GW⓾-N⓸

Y⓾L-G㋤-ⓔ ㋤-S⓾-Y⓪

I have nothing to declare.

저는 세관신고를 할것이 없어요.

J⓾-N⓸ Sⓔ-GWⓐN-SH①N-GG⓪-R⓸L

HⓐL-G⓾-SH㋤ ⓾P-S⓾-Y⓪

I'm here on business.

저는 사업 때문에 왔어요

J⓾-N⓸ Sⓐ-⓾P Dⓐ-M⓸-ⓔ

Wⓐ-S⓾-Y⓪

I'm now on vacation.

저는 지금 휴가중이예요

J⓾-N⓸ J㋤-G⓸M

HY⓸-Gⓐ J⓸NG ㋤-Yⓔ-Y⓪

Is there a problem?

무슨 문제가 있나요?

M⓸-S⓸N M⓸N-Jⓔ-Gⓐ

①N-Nⓐ-Y⓪

PHRASEMAKER

To use this simple phrasemaker,
name the accommodations
you are looking for and then go to the bottom of
the page and say...Jⓘ-NⓐL-Gⓤh-Yⓔ-Yⓞ

▶ **One night...**

하룻밤...

Hⓐh-Ⓡⓞⓞ-PⓐhM...

▶ **Two nights...**

이틀밤...

ⒺⒺ-TⓞⓤL-BBⓐhM...

▶ **One week...**

일주일...

ⓘL-Jⓞⓞ-ⓘL...

▶ **Two weeks...**

이주...

ⒺⒺ-Jⓞⓞ...

...I'll be staying.

저는 ~지낼거예요.

...Jⓘ-NⓐL-Gⓤh-Yⓔ-Yⓞ

USEFUL PHRASES

I need a porter.

저는 짐을 옮길사람이 필요해요

J(uh)-N(oo)N   J(i)M-(oo)L
(O)LM-G(i)L-S(ah)-R(ah)-M(EE)
P(i)-RY(O)-H(a)-Y(O)

These are my bags.

제가방들이예요

J(e)   G(ah)-B(ah)NG-D(oo)-
R(EE)-Y(e)-Y(O)

I'm missing a bag.

저는 가방을 잃어 버렸어요

J(uh)-N(oo)N   G(ah)-B(ah)NG-(oo)L   (EE)-R(uh)
B(uh)-RY(uh)-SS(uh)-Y(O)

Thank you.

감사해요

G(ah)M-S(ah)-H(a)-Y(O)

PHRASEMAKER

To say **Where is...?**, name
what you are looking for then
go to the bottom of the page and say ...ⓤⓗ-DⒺⒺ-ⓔ̃
ⓘN-Nⓐⓗ-Yⓞ

▸ **Customs...**

세관...

SⒺ̃-GWⓐⓗN...

▸ **Baggage claim...**

수화물 찾는곳...

Sⓞⓞ-HWⓐⓗ-MⓞⓤL
CHⓐⓗ-NⓞⓤN-Gⓞ̃T...

▸ **Taxi stand...**

택시 타는 곳...

TⓐK-SⒺⒺ-ⓇⓞⓤL   Tⓐⓗ-NⓞⓤN-Gⓞ̃T...

▸ **The bus stop...**

버스 정류장...

Bⓤⓗ-Sⓞⓤ   JⓤⓗNG-NYⓞⓞ-JⓐⓗNG...

...where is?

~어디에 있나요?

...ⓤⓗ-DⒺⒺ-ⓔ̃   ⓘN-Nⓐⓗ-Yⓞ

HOTEL SURVIVAL

A wide selection of accommodations is available in major cities. Hotels are divided into groups, e.g. super deluxe (SDL), deluxe (DLX), 1st class, 2nd class, and 3rd class. There is also the Yogwan (Korean style inn) and Minbok (Korean Home stay).

- Make reservations well in advance and request the address of the hotel to be written in Korean as most taxi drivers do not speak English.

- Always have identification ready when checking in.

- Do not leave valuables or cash in your room when you are not there!

- Electrical items like blow-dryers may be provided by your hotel; however, you may want to purchase small electrical appliances there.

- It is a good idea to make sure you give your room number to persons you expect to call you. This can avoid confusion with western names.

KEY WORDS

Hotel
호텔
HO-TEL

Bellboy
벨보이
BEL-BO-EE

Maid
도우미
DO-oo-MEE

Message
메시지
ME-SSE-JEE

Reservation
예약
YE-YahK

Room service
룸서비스
ROOM-Suh-BEE-Sou

CHECKING IN

My name is...

제이름은...

Jℯ ⒺⒺ-Rⓞⓤ-Mⓞⓝ...

I have a reservation.

저는 예약을 했어요.

Jⓤⓗ-NⓞⓤN Yℯ Yⓐⓗ-Gⓞⓤ Hⓐ̆-Sⓤⓗ-Yⓞ

Have you any vacancies?

방이 있나요?

BⓐⓗNG-ⒺⒺ ⒾN-Nⓐⓗ-Yⓞ

What is the charge per night?

하룻밤 가격이 어떻게 되지요?

Hⓐⓗ-RⓞⓤT-PPⓐⓗM
Gⓐⓗ-KYⓤⓗ-GⒺⒺⓤ-DDⓤⓗ-Kℯ
DⒶ-JⒺⒺ-Yⓞ

Please give me my room key.

제 방키를 주세요.

Jℯ BⓐⓗNG-KⒺⒺ-RⓞⓤL
Jⓞⓞ-Sℯ-Yⓞ

PHRASEMAKER

The Korean phrase literally translates to "I **(a bath)** want a room with". Closed parentheses in the EPLS transliteration holds the place for the object to be inserted.

▶ **A bath...**

욕실(이)...

(YOK-SHiL)

▶ **One bed...**

침대하나(가)...

(CHiM-Dē-Gah Hah-Nah)

▶ **Two beds...**

침대두개(가)...

(CHiM-Dē-Gah Too-Gē)

▶ **A shower...**

H샤워기(가)...M

(SHah-Wuh KEE Gah)

I...want a room with.

저는 ~있는방을 원해요

Juh-Non (YOK-SHiL) EEN-Non
Pahng-oL Wuhn-HA-YO

USEFUL PHRASES

My room key, please.

제 방키를 주세요

Jⓔ BⓐNG-KⒺⒺ-RⓞⓤL
Jⓞⓞ-Sⓔ-Yⓞ

Are there any messages for me?

저한테 남겨진메시지가 있나요?

JⓤH-HⓐN-Tⓔ NⓐM-GYⓤH-JⓘN-
Mⓔ-SSⓔ-JⒺⒺ-Gⓐh ⓘN-Nⓐh-Yⓞ

Where is the dining room?

식사 하는곳은 어디에 있나요?

SHⓘK-Sⓐh Hⓐh-NⓞⓤN-GⓄ-SⓞⓤN
ⓤh-DⒺⒺ-ⓔ ⓘN-Nⓐh-Yⓞ

Are meals included?

식사도 포함되어있나요?

SHⓘK-Sⓐh-DⓄ PⓄ-HⓐhM-
DⒶ-ⓤh ⓘN-Nⓐh-Yⓞ

What time is breakfast?

아침은 몇시에 먹나요?

ⓐh-CHⓘ-MⓞⓤN MYⓤh-SSHⒺⒺ-ⓔ
Yⓔ-Mⓐh K-Nⓐh-Yⓞ

WAKE UP CALL

Please wake me at 6:00 a.m.

아침 여섯시에 깨워주세요.

@-CH①M Y⑩-S⑩-SSH㊤-ê
G㋡-W⑩-J⑳-Sê-Y⓪

Please wake me at 6:30 a.m.

아침 여섯시 반에 깨워주세요.

@-CH①M Y⑩-S⑩-SSH㊤ B@-Nê
G㋡-W⑩-J⑳-Sê-Y⓪

Please wake me at 7:00 a.m.

아침 일곱시에 깨워주세요.

@-CH①M ①L-G⓪P-SSH㊤-ê
G㋡-W⑩-J⑳-Sê-Y⓪

Please wake me at 7:30 a.m.

아침 일곱시 반에 깨워주세요.

@-CH①M ①L-G⓪P-SSH㊤-B@-Nê
G㋡-W⑩-J⑳-Sê-Y⓪

Please wake me a 8:00 a.m.

아침 여덟시에 깨워주세요.

@-CH①M Y⑩-D⑩LB-SSH㊤-ê
G㋡-W⑩-J⑳-Sê-Y⓪

PHRASEMAKER

This phrasemaker visually reflects Korean word order, usually subject-object-verb. The English phrase **"I need toilet paper"** literally translates as "I **(toilet paper)** need" in Korean. Closed parentheses in the EPLS transliteration at the bottom of the next page holds the place for the object to be inserted.

▶ **A babysitter...**

베이비시터(가)...

(Bẽ-EE-Sⓘ-Tⓤⓗ)

▶ **A bellboy...**

벨보이(가)...

(BẽL-Bⓞ-EE)

▶ **More blankets...**

담요(가) 더...

(DⓐⓗM-Yⓞ-Gⓐⓗ)

▶ **Ice cubes...**

얼음(이)...

(ⓤⓗ-BⓞⓤM)

▶ **More towels...**

수건(이) ...

(Sⓞⓞ-GⓤⓗN-EE Dⓤⓗ)

▶ **An extra key...**

여분의열쇠(가)...

(Y⑩-B⑩N-⑩㋐)

▶ **A maid...**

도우미(가)...

(D⑩-⑩-M㋐)

▶ **The manager...**

메니져(가)...

(M㋐-N㋐-JY⑩)

▶ **Clean sheets...**

깨끗한 시트(가)...

(GG㋐-G⑩-T㋐N SH㋐-T⑩)

▶ **Soap...**

비누(가)...

(B㋐-N⑩)

▶ **Toilet paper...**

화장지(가)...

(HW㋐-J㋐NG-J㋐)

I ... need.

저는 ~필요해요

J⑩-N⑩N (HW㋐-J㋐NG-J㋐)

P⑩-RY⑩-H㋐-Y⑩

USEFUL PHRASES

(PROBLEMS)

There is no electricity.

전기가 없어요.

J⑩N-G㋛-G⒜   ⑩P-S⑩-Y⓪

There is no heat.

히터가 없어요.

H㋛-T⑩-G⒜   ⑩P-S⑩-Y⓪

There is no hot water.

다뜨거운물이 없어요.

DD⑩-G⑩-⑩N   M⑩-R㋛
⑩P-S⑩-Y⓪

There is no light.

전등이 없어요.

J⑩N-D⑩NG-㋛   ⑩P-S⑩-Y⓪

There is no toilet paper.

화장지가 없어요.

HW⒜-J⒜NG-J㋛-G⒜   ⑩P-S⑩-Y⓪

PHRASEMAKER

(SPECIAL NEEDS)

▸ **An elevator...**

엘리베이터(가)...

ⓔL-ㅓⒺⒺ-Bⓔ-ⒺⒺ-Tⓤⓗ...

▸ **A wheelchair...**

휠체어...

HWⒺⒺL-CHⓔ-ⓤⓗ...

▸ **Facilities for the disabled...**

장애인을 위한 기구(가)...

JⓐⓗNG-ⓔ-ⓘN-ⓞⓞL ⓞⓞⓤr L

WⒺⒺ-HⓐⓗN GⒺⒺ-Gⓞⓞ...

...do you have?

~있나요?

...ⓘN-Nⓐⓗ-Yⓞ

Note: Accessability for the disabled in Korea is limited.

CHECKING OUT

The bill, please.

계산서 주세요.

G(e)-S(ah)N-S(ah)

J(oo)-S(e)-Y(O)

There is a mistake!

오차가 있습니다!

(O)-CH(ah)-G(ah)

Do you accept credit cards?

크래딧 카드를 받나요?

K(ou)-R(a)-D(i)T K(ah)-D(ou)-R(ou)L

B(ah)N-N(ah)-Y(O)

Please bring my luggage.

제짐을 가지고 와주세요.

J(e)-J(i)M-(ou)L J(O)M

G(ah)-J(i)-G(O)

W(ah)-J(oo)-S(e)-Y(O)

Please call a taxi.

택시를 잡아주세요.

TĀK-SEE-RᵒᵘL Jₐₕ-Bₐₕ-Jᵒᵒ-Sᵉ-YO

I had a very good time!

좋은 시간이였어요!

JO-ᵒᵘN-SHEE-GₐₕN-
EE-Yᵘʰ-Sᵘʰ-YO

Thank you very much.

대단히 감사합니다.

Dā-DₐₕN-HEE
GₐₕM-Sₐₕ-HₐₕM-NEE-Dₐₕ

See you next time.

다음에 또 만나요.

Dₐₕ-ᵒᵘ-Mᵉ DDO MₐₕN-Nₐₕ-YO

Good-bye (Said to the person staying as you leave.)

안녕히 계세요.

ₐₕ-NYᵘʰNG-HEE Gᵉ-Sᵉ-YO

Good-bye (Said to the person leaving.)

안녕히 가세요.

ₐₕN-NYᵘʰNG-HEE
Gₐₕ-Sᵉ-YO

RESTAURANT SURVIVAL

Korean cuisine is diverse, and you will find many different foods and dishes to enjoy. Dishes consist of several meat and fish dishes accompanied with vegetables and greens.

- You will find many different cuisines in Korea, e.g. Korean, Chinese, Western including some familiar foreign restaurant chains and fast food restaurants.

- Street carts offer snack foods at economical prices.

- At meals, Koreans offer glasses of liquor to each other as a gesture of friendship.

- When elderly dinner participants are in attendance, try to keep the same eating pace that they set.

- Tipping is not customary in Korea but is accepted for exceptional service.

KEY WORDS

Breakfast

아침

@ah-CH@iM

Lunch

점심

J@uhM-SH@iM

Dinner

저녁

J@uh-NY@uhK

Waiter

웨이터

W@ĕ-@EE-T@uh

Waitress

웨이트레스

W@ĕ-@EE-T@ou-L@ĕ-S@ou

Restaurant

식당

SH@iK-D@ahNG

USEFUL PHRASES

A table for...

안즐 자리 주세요...

...ⓐN-JⓞL-Jⓐ-Rⓔ Jⓞ-Sⓔ-Yⓞ

2 (persons)	**4** (persons)	**6** (persons)
두명	네명	여섯명
Dⓞ-MYⓐNG	Nⓔ-MYⓐNG	Yⓐ-Sⓤ)T-MYⓐNG

The menu, please.

메뉴를 주세요.

Mⓔ-NYⓞ-Rⓞ)L Jⓞ-Sⓔ-Yⓞ

Separate checks, please.

계산서를 따로 주세요.

Gⓔ-Sⓐ)N-Sⓤ)-Rⓞ)L DDⓐ-Rⓞ
Jⓞ-Sⓔ-Yⓞ

We are in a hurry.

우리가 지금 좀 서두르고 있어요.

ⓞ-Rⓔ-Gⓐ Jⓔ-Gⓤ)M
JⓞM Sⓤ)-Dⓞ-Rⓞ)-Gⓞ
ⓔ-SSⓐ-Yⓞ

What do you recommend?

추천하는 음식이 무어십니까?

CHⓞⓞ-CHⓤⓗN-Hⓐⓗ-NⓞⓤN
ⓞⓤM-SHⓘ-Gⓔⓔ Mⓞⓞ-ⓤⓗ-SHⓘM-Nⓔⓔ-GGⓐⓗ

Please bring me...

저에게 ~가져다 주세요.

...Jⓤⓗ-ⓔ̃-Gⓔ̃ Gⓐⓗ-JYⓤⓗ-Dⓐⓗ
Jⓞⓞ-Sⓔ̃-Yⓞ

Please bring us...

우리에게 ~가져다 주세요.

...ⓞⓞ-R̰ⓔⓔ-ⓔ̃-Gⓔ̃ Gⓐⓗ-JYⓤⓗ-Dⓐⓗ
Jⓞⓞ-Sⓔ̃-Yⓞ

I'm hungry.

배가 고파요.

Bⓐ̃-Gⓐⓗ Gⓞ-Pⓐⓗ-Yⓞ

I'm thirsty.

목이 말라요.

Mⓞⓞ-Gⓔⓔ MⓐⓗL-Lⓐⓗ-Yⓞ

The bill, please.

계산서 주세요.

Gⓔ̃-SⓐⓗN-Sⓤⓗ Jⓞⓞ-Sⓔ̃-Yⓞ

KOREAN CUISINES AND STYLES

Rice is a staple food in the Korean menu. Many dishes mix rice with beans, barley cereals, and chestnuts. There are many different combinations that reinvent rice.

Kimchi, "fermented spiced cabbage," is a very common accompaniment to meals. There are other fermented varieties, each with a specific flavor. This dish is highly nutritious.

Korea has all kinds of eating establishments, ranging from pojangmachas (street vendors) and hole-in-the-wall restaurants to high-priced, formal restaurants with full-course meals.

Additionally, you can find many types of medium-sized places to eat offering a wide range of food types, including traditional Korean food, fast food, Western and other non-Korean dishes.

Tipping is not customary in Korea but is accepted for exceptional service.

Etiquette: Your chopstick and spoon should not be held together in one hand and neither should be rested on bowls or dishes. Bowls should not be held in your hands. At the end of the meal, place the chopsticks and spoon where they were when they were first placed.

DRINKING ESTABLISHMENTS

Tea Houses

Traditional tea-houses offer wonderful teas, elegant decor, and an excellent way to experience Korea. Some offer entertainment and provide a unique and memorable experience.

Drink

With their meals, Koreans rarely drink anything but a little water or boricha (barley tea). Tea and coffee shops abound. The most popular common drinks include soju makgulli (liquor) and dong-dong-ju.

Bars

Drinking establishments range from the same pojangmachas, where you can eat, to upscale night clubs with expensive table charges. In between are a variety of bars, pubs, and rock cafes.

Koreans offer glasses of liquor to each other as a gesture of friendship. Even if you don't usually drink, it is courteous to drink at least the first glass when you attend a drinking round so as not to ruin the drinking mood.

BEVERAGE LIST

Coffee

거피

K(uh)-P(EE)

Decaffeinated coffee

카페인 없는 커피

K(ah)-P(ĕ)-(i)N   (uh)B-N(ou)N   K(uh)-P(EE)

Tea

차

CH(ah)

Cream

크림

K(ou)-R̰(EE)M

Sugar

설탕

S(uh)L-T(ah)NG

Lemon

레몬

L(ĕ)-M(O)N

Milk

우유

OO-YOO

Hot chocolate

코코아

KO-KO-ah

Juice

주스

JOO-Sou

Orange juice

오렌지 주스

O-REN-JEE   JOO-Sou

Ice water

얼음 물

uh-ROOM   MOOL

Mineral water

미네랄 워터

MEE-Ne-RahL   Wuh-Tuh

Ice

얼음

uh-ROOM

AT THE BAR

Bartender

바텐더

B⒜-T⒠N-D⒜

Cocktail

칵테일

K⒜K-T⒠-⒤L

With ice

얼음도 같이 주세요

⒜-D⒰M-D⓪ K⒜-CH⒠
J⓪-S⒠-Y⓪

No ice

얼음 없이 주세요

⒜-D⒰M-D⓪ ⒜P-SH⒠
J⓪-S⒠-Y⓪

With lemon

레몬도 같이 주세요

L⒠-M⓪N D⓪ K⒜-CH⒠
J⓪-S⒠-Y⓪

PHRASEMAKER

▶ **Champagne...**
샴페인
SH@M-P®-①N...

▶ **Beer...**
맥주
M@K-J@...

▶ **Wine...**
포도주
P◎-D◎-J@...

▶ **Red wine**
적포도주
J@K-P◎-D◎-J@...

▶ **White wine**
백포도주
B@K-P◎-D◎-J@...

...I would like a glass of.
~한잔 주세요.

...H@N-J@N J@-S®-Y◎

FAMILIAR FOODS

On the following pages you will
find lists of foods you are familiar
with, along with other information
such as basic utensils and preparation
instructions.

A polite way to get a waiter's or waitress's attention
is to say Y⑩-JJ⑩-P⑩-D⑩ DW⑤L-GG⑩-Y⑩, which means
May I ask?, followed by your request and thank you.

May I ask?

여쭈어봐도 될까요?

Y⑩-JJ⑩-P⑩-D⑩ DW⑤L-GG⑩-Y⑩

Please bring me...

~(을/를) 갔다주세요

...J⑩-S⑤-Y⑩

Thank you.

감사합니다.

K⑩M-S⑩-H⑩M-N⑤-D⑩

STARTERS

Appetizer

에피타이저

ⓔ-Pⓔⓔ-Tⓐⓗ-ⓔⓔ-Jⓤⓗ

Bread and butter

빵과 버터

PPⓐⓗNG-GGWⓐⓗ Bⓐⓗ-Tⓤⓗ

Cheese

치즈

CHⓔⓔ-Jⓞⓤ

Fruit

과일

GWⓐⓗ-ⓘL

Salad

샐러드

Sⓐ-Lⓤⓗ-Dⓞⓤ

Soup

수프

Sⓞⓞ-Pⓞⓤ

MEATS

Bacon

베이컨

BĒ-EE-KⓊN

Beef

쇠고기

SWĒ-GⓄ-GEE

Beef Steak

스테이크

SⓄⓊ-TĒ-EE-KⓄⓊ

Ham

햄

HâM

Lamb

양고기

Yâ NG-GⓄ-GEE

Pork

돼지고기

TWĒ-JEE-GⓄ-GEE

POULTRY

Baked chicken

닭고기 구이

D@LK-GG⊙-G🄴🄴

Grilled

그릴한

G⊚⊚-Ⓡ①L-H@N

Fried chicken

후라이드 치킨

H⊚⊚-Ⓡ@-🄴🄴-D⊚ᵘ CH🄴🄴-K①N

Duck

오리

⊙-Ⓡ🄴🄴

Goose

거위

G⓾-W🄴🄴

Turkey

칠면조

CH①L-MY⓾N-J⊙

SEAFOOD

Fish

생선

S@NG-S⑩N

Lobster

바닷가재

B@-D@T-G@-J@

Oysters

굴

G⑳L

Salmon

연어

Y⑩N-N⑩

Shrimp

새우

S@-⑳

Tuna

참치

CH@M-CH⒠

OTHER ENTREES

Sandwich

샌드위치

SⓐN-Dⓞⓤ-Wⓔⓔ-CHⓔⓔ

Hot dog

핫도그

HⓐⓗT-Dⓞ-Gⓞⓤ

Hamburger

햄버거

HⓐM-Bⓤⓗ-Gⓤⓗ

French fries

프랜치 후라이

Pⓞⓤ-RⓐN-CHⓔⓔ Hⓞⓞ-Rⓐⓗ-ⓔⓔ

Pasta

파스타

Pⓐⓗ-Sⓞⓤ-Tⓐⓗ

Pizza

피자

Pⓔⓔ-Jⓐⓗ

VEGETABLES

Carrots

당근

D@NG-G@N

Corn

옥수수

@K-S@-S@

Mushroom

버섯

B@-S@T

Onion

양파

Y@NG-P@

Potato

감자

G@M-J@

Rice (cooked)

밥

P@P

Tomato

토마토

T@-M@-T@

FRUITS

Apple

사과

S@h-GW@h

Banana

바나나

B@h-N@h-N@h

Grape

포도

P◎-D◎

Lemon

레몬

L@ě-M◎N

Orange

오렌지

◎-Ř@ĕN-J@ĒĒ

Strawberry	**Watermelon**
딸기	수박
DD@hL-GG@ĒĒ	S◎◎-B@hK

DESSERT

Dessert

후식 / 디저트

H◎-SH①K / D㋱-J⒰-T⒪

Apple pie

애플 파이

㋐-P⒰L P㋔-㋱

Cherry pie

체리 파이

CH㋓-R㋱ P㋔-㋱

Pastry

패이스트리

P㋐-㋱-S⒪-T⒪-R㋱

Candy

사탕

S㋔-T㋔NG

Ice cream

아이스크림

@-EE-S@-K@-BEEM

Ice cream cone

아이스크림 콘

@-EE-S@-K@-BEEM K@N

Chocolate

초콜렛

CH@-K@-LL@T

Strawberry

딸기

DD@L-G@

Vanilla

바닐라

B@-N@L-L@

CONDIMENTS

Butter

버터

B⓾-T⓾

Ketchup

케첩

K⑧-CH⓾P

Mayonnaise

마요네즈

Mⓐ-YO-N⑧-J⓸

Mustard

겨자

GY⓾-Jⓐ

Salt

소금

SO-G⓸M

Pepper (black)

후추

H⓸-CH⓸

Sugar

설탕

S⓾L-TⓐNG

SETTINGS

Cup

컵

K(uh)P

Glass (drinking)

유리잔

Y(oo)-R(EE)-J(ah)N

Spoon

숟가락

S(oo)T-G(ah)-R(ah)K

Fork

포크

P(O)-K(ou)

Knife

칼

K(ah)L

Plate	**Napkin**
접시	냅킨
J(uh)P-SH(EE)	N(a)P-K(i)N

HOW DO YOU
WANT IT COOKED?

Baked

구운

G⑳-W⑳N

Grilled

그릴한

K⑳-ⓇⓘL-Hⓐ N

Steamed

찐

JJⓘN

Fried

튀긴

TⒺⒺ-Gⓘ N   Gⓐ

Medium

미디엄

MⒺⒺ-DⒺⒺ-⑳M

Well done, please.

푹익혀주세요

P⑳K-ⒺⒺ-KYⓤ-J⑳-Sⓔ-Yⓞ

PROBLEMS

This is not the food I ordered.

제가 주문한 음식이 아니예요.

Jŭ-Gah Joo-Moon-Han-oom-SHi-Gee ah-Nee-Yŭ-Yo

Please check my bill.

제 계산서를 좀 봐주세요.

Jŭ Gŭ-Sahn-Suh BWah-Joo-Sŭ-Yo

PRAISE

Thank you for the delicious meal.

맛있는식사 감사드려요.

Maht-EEN-Noun SHik-SSah Gahm-Sah Dou-Byuh-Yo

GETTING AROUND

Getting around in a foreign
country can be an adventure
in itself! Taxi and bus drivers
do not always speak English, so
it is essential to be able to give
simple directions. The words
and phrases in this chapter will
help you get to where you're going.

- Subway stations usually have maps for
  travelers. You can purchase your ticket at
  the ticket window. Fares are determined
  by destination. It is important to know
  that Korean Won or T-money are the only
  forms of payment accepted.

- You can purchase a T-money card at local
  vendors and use it on the bus or subway.
  You can refill your T-money card at kiosks
  or convenience stores advertising the sale
  of the T-money card.

- Taxis are abundant and economical. You
  will find taxi stands in the city.

- Have a map or the address that you want
  to go to written down in Korean.

- Remember to take a business card from
  your hotel to give to the taxi driver on
  your return.

- Carry your ID with you at all times while
  in Korea.

KEY WORDS

Airport

공항

G◎NG-H@NG

Bus Station

버스 정거장

B@-S◎ J@NG-G@-J@NG

Car Rental Agency

렌트카

R@N-T◎-K@

Taxi Stand

택시 정류장

T@K-S© J@NG-BY◎-J@NG

Train Station

기차역

G©-CH@-Y@K

AIR TRAVEL

Airport

공항

GONG-HahNG

A one-way ticket, please.

편도 표로 주세요.

PYuhN-DO-PYO-RO   JOO-Seh-YO

A round trip ticket, please.

왕복표로 주세요.

WahNG-BOK-PYO-RO
JOO-Seh-YO

First class

일등석

iL-DouNG-SahK

How much do I owe?

얼마입니까?

ahL-Mah   iM-NEE-Kah

Gate

게이트

Geh-EE-Tou

PHRASEMAKER

Say what you need and then
go to the bottom of the page and
say ...WⓤN-Ⓗ-Ⓐ-Yⓞ.

▸ **A first class seat...**

일등석(을)...

ⒾL-DDⓞⓤNG-Sⓤ뷔K...

▸ **A seat next to the window...**

창가 쪽 자리(를)...

CHⓐⓗNG-GGⓐⓗ-JJⓄK-JJⓐⓗ-ℝⒺⒺ...

▸ **A seat on the aisle...**

통로 쪽 자리(를)...

TⓄNG-ℝⓄ-JJⓄK-JJⓐⓗ-ℝⒺⒺ...

▸ **A seat near the exit...**

출구 근처 자리(를)...

CHⓄⓄL-GⓞⓤN CHⓤⓗ-Jⓐⓗ-ℝⒺⒺ...

...I would like.

~원해요.

...WⓤN-Ⓗ-Ⓐ-Yⓞ

BY BUS

Bus

버스

B⓾-S⓸

Where is the bus stop?

버스 정류장은 어디에 있나요?

B⓾-S⓸ J⓾NG-BY⓸-J⓪NG-⓸N
⓾-D⓺-ĕ-①N-N⓪-Y⓪

Do you go to...?

~로 가나요?

...B⓪ G⓪-N⓪-Y⓪

What is the fare?

운임 얼마예요?

⓸N-①-M⓺ ⓪L-M⓪-Yĕ-Y⓪

Do I need exact change?

정확한잔액이필요 한가요?

CH⓪NG-HW⓪K-H⓪N
J⓪N-ĕ-G⓺
P①-BY⓪-H⓪N-G⓪-Y⓪

PHRASEMAKER

Say where you want to go
then go to the bottom of the page and say...
...G@h-N@N B@h-S@-G@h @h-DD@h-G@h-SH©-JY©.

▸ **to the beach?**

바닷가로...

P@h-T@h-GG@h...

▸ **to the market?**

마켓 / 시장으로...

SH©-J@hNG...

▸ **to the airport?**

공항으로...

G©NG-H@hNG...

▸ **to the train station?**

기차역으로...

G©-CH@h-Y@hK...

Which bus goes...

~가는 버스가 어떤 것이죠?

...G@h-N@N B@h-S@-G@h
@h-DD@h-G@h-SH©-JY©

BY CAR

Can you help me?

도와줄수 있나요?

PⓄ-Wⓐⓗ-JⓞⓞL-SSⓞⓞ ⓘN-Nⓐⓗ-YⓄ

My car won't start.

제 자동차가 안움직여요.

Jⓔ Jⓐⓗ-DⓄNG CHⓐⓗ-Gⓐⓗ

ⓐⓗ-NⓞⓞM-Jⓘ-GYⓤⓗ-YⓄ

Can you fix it?

고쳐줄수 있나요?

GⓄ-CHYⓤⓗ-JⓞⓞL-Sⓞⓞ ⓘN-Nⓐⓗ-YⓄ

What will it cost?

얼마나 드나요?

ⓤⓗL-Mⓐⓗ-Nⓐⓗ Dⓞⓤ-Nⓐⓗ-YⓄ

How long will it take?

얼마나 오래 걸리나요?

ⓤⓗL-Mⓐⓗ-Nⓐⓗ Ⓞ-Rãⓐ

GⓤⓗL-Lⓔⓔ-Nⓐⓗ-YⓄ

PLEASE CHECK

Please check the battery.

배터리(를) 확인해보세요.

BBⓐʰ-DDⓐ-Ⓡ EE

HWⓐʰ-GⒾN-Mⓐ-BⓄ-Sⓔ-YⓄ

Please check the brakes.

브레이크(를) 확인해 보세요.

Bᵒᵘ-Ⓡ ⓔ-EE-Kᵒᵘ

HWⓐʰ-GⒾN-Mⓐ-BⓄ-Sⓔ-YⓄ

Please check the oil.

오일/기름(을) 확인해보세요.

Ⓞ-ⒾL   GEE-Ⓡ ᵒᵘM

HWⓐʰ-GⒾN-Mⓐ-BⓄ-Sⓔ-YⓄ

Please check the tires.

타이어(를) 확인해보세요.

Tⓐʰ-EE-ᵘʰ

HWⓐʰ-GⒾN-Mⓐ-BⓄ-Sⓔ-YⓄ

Please check the water.

물(을) 확인해보세요.

MᵒᵒL

HWⓐʰ-GⒾN-Mⓐ-BⓄ-Sⓔ-YⓄ

SUBWAYS AND TRAINS

Where is the train station?

기차역은 어디에 있나요?

GEE-CHah-YuhK-GouN

uh-DEE-ĕ iN-Nah-YO

A one-way ticket, please.

편도선표로 주세요.

PYuhN-DO-SuhN

PYO-BO Joo-Sĕ-YO

A round trip ticket, please.

왕복표로 주세요.

Wah NG-BOK-PYO-BO

Joo-Sĕ-YO

First class seat

일등석

iL-DDouNG-SuhK

Second class seat

이등석

EE-DDouNG-SuhK

How much is the fare?

운임이 어떻게 되나요?

@N-@-DD@-K@ DW@-N@-Y@

Is this seat taken?

이 자리는 잡혔나요?

@-J@-R@-N@N
J@P-PY@N-N@-Y@

Do I have to change trains?

기차를 바꾸어 타야하나요?

G@-CH@-R@L B@-GG@-@
T@-Y@-H@-N@-Y@

Where are we?

우리는 지금 어디에 있나요?

@-R@-N@N
J@-G@M @-D@-@
@N-N@-Y@

BY TAXI

Please call a taxi.

택시를 불러주세요.

T@K-S@E-R@L
B@L-L@h-J@-S@-Y@

Can you come now?

지금 와줄수 있나요?

J@E-G@M-W@h-J@L-S@-
@N-N@h-Y@

I want to go to...

~로 가고 싶어요.

...G@h-G@-SH@-P@h-Y@

Stop here, please.

여기서 멈춰주세요.

Y@h-G@E-S@h   M@hM-CH@h   J@-S@-Y@

Please wait.

기다려주세요.

G@E-D@h-RY@h   J@-S@-Y@

How much do I owe?

얼마입니까?

@hL-M@h-@M-N@E-GG@h

Take me to this address, please.

이 주소로 가주세요.

Ⓔ J⓪⓪-S⓪-R⓪
Gⓐⓗ-J⓪⓪-Sⓔ-Y⓪

Have someone at your hotel write down the address for you in Korean.

Take me to this hotel, please.

이 호텔로 가주세요.

Ⓔ H⓪-Tⓔ⌐L-L⓪
Gⓐⓗ-J⓪⓪-Sⓔ-Y⓪

Take me to the airport, please.

공항으로 가주세요.

G⓪NG-HⓐⓗNG-⓪ⓤ-R⓪
Gⓐⓗ-J⓪⓪-Sⓔ-Y⓪

Take me to the subway station, please.

전철역으로 가주세요.

JⓤⓗN-CHⓤⓗL-YⓤⓗK-⓪ⓤ-R⓪
Gⓐⓗ-J⓪⓪-Sⓔ-Y⓪

SHOPPING

Whether you plan a major shopping spree or just need to purchase some basic necessities, the following information is useful.

- Shopping hours in Korea are varied and many shops stay open as late as midnight.

- Seoul offers great shopping for all, from souvenir shops to department stores. From luxury to trendy, you will find a wide variety of items to choose from.

- Apgujung is an upper class hub of Seoul encompassing fashionable boutiques, Korea's Rodeo Drive, and the famous Galleria Department Store.

- Department stores, shops, and restaurants at tourist destinations usually accept credit cards; however, small stores usually accept cash only.

- Duty-free Korea has outlet stores which offer deeper discounts.

- Tax-free shops will provide tax refund information to buyers.

- Money exchange receipts should be kept in order to change money back when leaving Korea.

KEY WORDS

Credit card

크래딧 카드

K◍-R◉-D◉T K◍-D◍

Money

돈

D◉N

Receipt

영수증

Y◍NG-S◍-J◍NG

Sale

세일 / 할인

SS◉-◉L / H◍-R◉N

Store

가게

G◍-G◉

Traveler's check

여행자 수표

Y◉-H◍NG-J◍ S◍-PY◉

USEFUL PHRASES

Do you sell...?

~ 파나요?

...P⒜-N⒜-Y◎

Do you have...?

~ 있나요?

...①N-N⒜-Y◎

I want to buy.

사고싶어요.

S⒜-G◎-SH①-P⒰-Y◎

How much?

얼마인가요?

⒰L-M⒜   ①N-G⒜-Y◎

What time is the shop open?

가게가 몇시에 여나요?

G⒜-Gⓔ-G⒜   MY⒰T-SSHⒺⒺ-ⓔ

Y⒰-N⒜-Y◎

It's all right.

괜찮습니다.

GWⓐN-CHⓐN-SSⓞⓤM-Lⓔⓔ-Dⓐh

I´m just looking.

구경하고 있어요.

Gⓞⓞ-NYⓐhNG

Pⓞ-Gⓞ-ⓔⓔ-Sⓤhh-YⓄ

Is it very expensive?

아주 비싼가요?

ⓐh-Jⓞⓞ Bⓔⓔ-SSⓐhN-Gⓐh-YⓄ

Can you give make it cheaper?

싸게 해줄수 있나요?

SSⓐh-Gⓔ̆ Hⓐ̃-JⓞⓞL-Sⓞⓞ

ⓘN-Nⓐh-YⓄ

I'll buy it.

살께요.

SⓐhL-GGⓔ̆-YⓄ

I'd like a receipt, please.

영수증을 주세요.

YⓤhNG-Sⓞⓞ-JⓞⓤNG-ⓞⓤL

Jⓞⓞ-Sⓔ̆-YⓄ

SHOPS AND SERVICES

Bakery

빵집

PP@NG-J①P

Bank

은행

⑩N-H@NG

Beauty salon / Barbershop

미용실 / 이발소

M①E-Y①NG-SH①L / ①E-B@L-S①

Jewelry store

보석상

B①-S@K-S@NG

Bookstore

책방

CH@K-PP@NG

Camera shop

카메라 가게

K@-M①-R@ K@-G①

Pharmacy

약국

Y@K-G⑩K

SHOPPING LIST

On the following pages you will find some common items you may need to purchase on your trip.

Aspirin

아스피린

@h-S@u-P①-Ⓡ①N

Cigarettes

담배

D@hM-B@a

Deodorant

디오드런트

D©©-①-D@u-Ⓡ@hN-T@u

Dress

드레스

D@u-Ⓡ©e-S@u

Film (camera)

필름

P①-L@uM

Perfume

향수

HY@NG-S⑩

Razor blade

면도날

MY⑩N-D⓪-N@L

Shampoo

샴푸

SH@M-P⑩

Shaving cream

면도용 크림

MY⑩N-D⓪-Y⓪NG   K⑩-B⑯M

Shirt

셔츠

SH@-SS⑩

Sunglasses

선글라스

S⑩N-G⑩L-L@-S⑩

Suntan lotion

썬텐 로션

SS(uh)N-T(e)N L(o)-SH(uh)N

Toothbrushes

칫솔

CH(i)-SS(o)L

Toothpaste

치약

CH(i)-Y(ah)K

Water (bottled)

물

M(oo)L

Water (mineral)

미네랄 워터

M(ee)-N(e)-R(ah)L W(uh)-T(uh)

ESSENTIAL SERVICES

THE BANK

As a traveler in a foreign country your primary contact with banks will be to exchange money.

- The official Korean currency is the Won. The Won is divided into W10,000, 5,000 and 1,000 notes. Coins are in five hundred, one hundred, fifty, and ten won denominations.

- Currency can be changed at banks, which are usually open Monday through Friday between 9:30 AM and 4:30 PM.

- Hotels and exchange service centers also change currency. Hotels usually offer 24 hour service. Exchange centers are usually open from 9:30 AM to 10 PM daily.

- ATM's are not always convenient. Check with your bank to see if your card is accepted and get exact locations.

- ATM/CD or cash dispensers only offering cash are located in busy areas like subways, bus, rail stations and convenience stores. They usually post English directions.

KEY WORDS

Bank

은행

@N-H@NG

Exchange bureau

환전소

HW@N-J@N-S@

Money

돈

D@N

Traveler's check

여행자 수표

Y@-H@NG-J@ S@-PY@

Note: Use a calculator when changing money, check your transaction right away, and make sure to get a receipt.

USEFUL PHRASES

Where is the bank?

은행이 어디에 있나요?

ⓞⓤN-HⓐNG-Ⓔ   ⓤh-DⒺⒺ-ⓔ
ⓘN-Nⓐh-Yⓞ

When does the bank open?

은행은 언제 여나요?

ⓞⓤN-HⓐNG-ⓞⓤN   ⓤhN-Jⓔ
Yⓤh-Nⓐh-Yⓞ

Where is the exchange office?

환전소는 어디에 있나요?

HWⓐN-JⓤhN-SⓞN-NⓞⓤN
ⓤh-DⒺⒺ-ⓔ   ⓘN-Nⓐh-Yⓞ

When does the exchange office open?

환전소는 언제 여나요?

HWⓐN-JⓤhN-SⓞN-NⓞⓤN
ⓤhN-Jⓔ   Yⓤh-Nⓐh-Yⓞ

Can I change dollars here?

달러를 여기서 환전할수 있나요?

DⓐL-Lⓤh-RⓞⓤL   Yⓤh-GⒺⒺ-Sⓤh
HWⓐN-JⓤhN-HⓐL-Sⓞⓞ   ⓘN-Nⓐh-Yⓞ

What is the exchange rate?

환율이 어떻게 되나요?

HW@N-Y00-R€€

@-DD@-K€

DW€-N@-Y0

Give me large bills.

액수가 큰 돈으로 주세요.

@K-S00-G@   K0N

D0N-@-R0

J00-S€-Y0

Give me smaller change.

잔돈으로 바꿔주세요.

J@N-D0N-@-R0

B@-GGW@-J00-S€-Y0

Do you have an ATM?

현금출납기가 있나요?

HY@N-G0M

CH00L-L@P-G€€-G@

0N-N@-Y0

POST OFFICE

If you are planning on sending letters and postcards, be sure to send them early so that you don't arrive home before they do.

KEY WORDS

Air mail

항공우편

K⓪P ⓞⓞ-PⒺⒺⓐN

Letter

편지

PⒺⒺⓤN Jⓔ

Post office

우체국

Wⓞⓞ-CHⓔ-Gⓞⓤ

Postcard

엽서

YⓤP-SSⓤ

Stamp

우표

ⓞⓞ-PYⓞ

USEFUL PHRASES

Where is the post office?

우체국은 어디에 있나요?

ⓞⓞ-CHⓔ-Gⓞⓞ-GⓞⓤN

ⓤⓗ-Dⓔⓔ-ⓔ ⓘN-Nⓐⓗ-Yⓞ

When does the post office open?

우체국은 언제 여나요?

ⓞⓞ-CHⓔ-Gⓞⓞ-GⓞⓤN

ⓤⓗN-Jⓔ Yⓤⓗ-Nⓐⓗ-Yⓞ

I need stamps.

우표가 필요해요.

ⓞⓞ-PYⓤⓗ-Gⓐⓗ

Pⓘ-RYⓞ-Hⓔ-Yⓞ

I need a postal envelope.

우편 봉투가 필요해요.

ⓞⓞ-PYⓤⓗN BⓞNG-Tⓞⓞ-Gⓐⓗ

Pⓘ-RYⓞ-Hⓔ-Yⓞ

I need a pen.

펜이 필요해요.

PⓔN-ⓔⓔ Pⓘ-RYⓞ-Hⓔ-Yⓞ

TELEPHONE

Placing phone calls in Korea can be
a test of will and stamina! Besides
the obvious language barriers, service
can vary greatly from one city to the
next.

- Cell phone rentals are available in Korea;
  however, in many cases, you must reserve
  ahead of your arrival.

- You can purchase pre-paid phone cards
  at convenience stores and news stands
  for use in card phones.

- There are credit card phones with which
  you can use your major credit cards to
  make a phone call.

- A third type of phone is the coin-operated
  telephone.

- You can find internet service at airports,
  train stations, and bus terminals. There are
  also a variety of internet cafes that offer
  internet service along with snacks and 24
  hour service.

KEY WORDS

Information (directory assistance)

114 (일일사)

ⓘL-ⓘL-SSⓐh

Long distance call

장거리 전화

JⓐNG-Gⓤh-RⒺⒺ JⓤhN-HWⓐh

Operator (telephone)

전화교환수

JⓤhN-HWⓐh-KYⓄ-HWⓐhN-Sⓞⓞ

Phone book

전화번호부

JⓤhN-HWⓐh-Bⓞⓞ

Public telephone

공중전화

KⓄNG-JⓞⓞNG-JⓤhN-HWⓐh

Telephone

전화

JⓤhN-HWⓐh

USEFUL PHRASES

Where is the telephone?

전화는 어디에 있나요?

J⒰N-HW⒜-N⒪N
⒰-D㋐-㋓ ⒤N-N⒜-Y⓪

Where is the public telephone?

공중전화는 어디에 있나요?

G⓪NG-J⒪NG-CH⒰N
HW⒜-N⒪N
⒰-D㋐-㋓ ⒤N-N⒜-Y⓪

May I use your telephone?

전화기를 빌려도 될까요?

J⒰N-HW⒜-R⒪L
B⒤L-LY⒰-D⓪ DW㋓-GG⒜-Y⓪

Operator, I don't speak Korean.

저는 한국말을 할줄 몰라요.

J⒰-N⒪N
H⒜N-G⓪NG-M⒜L-R⒪L
M⒜L-JJ⒪L

I want to call this number...

이 번호로 전화 하고싶어요.

EE-BⓊN-HO-RO　JⓊN-HWⓐ
Hⓐ-GO-SHⓘ-PⓊ-YO

1 일 ⓘL	2 이 EE	3 삼 SⓐM
4 사 Sⓐ	5 오 ⓞ	6 육 YⓄK
7 칠 CHⓘL	8 팔 PⓐL	9 구 GⓄ
✱	0 공/영 GⓄNG/YⓊNG	#

SIGHTSEEING AND ENTERTAINMENT

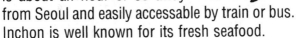

Korea is a peninsula located between China and Japan. Seoul is the capital of Korea. Inchon is a city located on the west coast of the country. It is about an hour or so away from Seoul and easily accessible by train or bus. Inchon is well known for its fresh seafood.

- Insadong is a neighborhood near downtown Seoul, known for its many galleries, pottery shops, and tea houses.

- There are two major outdoor markets in Seoul, Namdaemun and Dongdaemun. Namdaemun sells everything from socks to leather jackets. Tongdaemun is a smaller market with less selection.

- The **Kyongbokung Palace** grounds feature a beautiful 10-story stone pogoda from Kyongchonsa Temple.

KEY WORDS

Admission

입학

ⒺⒺP-HⓐⓗK

Map

지도

JⒺⒺ-Dⓞ

Reservation

예약

Yⓔ-YⓐⓗK

Ticket

표

PYⓞ

Tour

투어 / 관광

Tⓞⓞ-ⓤⓗ / GⓐⓗN-GWⓐⓗNG

Tour guide

투어/관광 가이드

Tⓞⓞ-ⓤⓗ GⓐⓗN-GWⓐⓗNG Gⓐⓗ-ⒺⒺ-Dⓞⓤ

USEFUL PHRASES

Where is the tourist agency?

여행사는 어디에 있나요?

Yⓤ-HⓐNG-SSⓐ-NⓞⓤN
ⓤ-DⒺⒺ-ⓔ ⓘN-Nⓐ-Yⓞ

Where do I buy a ticket?

표를 어디에서 구매하나요?

PYⓤ-RⓞⓤL ⓤ-DⒺⒺ-ⓔ-Sⓤ
Gⓞⓞ-Mⓐ-Hⓐ-Nⓐ-Yⓞ

How much?

얼마인가요?

ⓤL-Mⓐ-ⓘN-Gⓐ-Yⓞ

How long?

얼마나 걸리나요?

ⓤL-Mⓐ-Nⓐ GⓤL-LⒺⒺ-Nⓐ-Yⓞ

When?

언제요?

ⓤN-Jⓔ-Yⓞ

Where?

어디에서요?

ⓤ-DⒺⒺ-ⓔ-Sⓤ-Yⓞ

Do I need reservations?

예약이 필요 한가요?

YÉ-Yah-GEE Pï-RYO
Hah-N-Gah-YO

Does the guide speak English?

가이드가 영어를 하나요?

Gah-EE-Dou-Gah Yuh-NG-uh-Rou-L
Hah-Nah-YO

How much do children pay?

아이들은 얼마를 내나요?

ah-EE-Dou-Rou-N
uh-L-Mah-Rou-L
Nã-Nah-YO

We had fun.

우리는 즐거웠어요.

oo-REE-Nou-N Jou-L-Guh-Wuh-SSuh-YO

Thank you.

감사합니다.

Gah-M-Sah-Hah-M-NEE-Dah

PHRASEMAKER

- **a concert...**

콘서트...

(KⓄN-SSⓤⓗ-Tⓞⓤ)

- **a dance...**

댄스 클럽...

(DⓐN-SSⓞⓤ-KⓞⓤL-LⓤⓗB)

- **dinner...**

저녁식사...

(Jⓤⓗ-NYⓤⓗ-SSHⓘK-SSⓐⓗ)

- **the movie theater...**

영화관...

(YⓤⓗNG-HWⓐⓗ-GWⓐⓗN)

- **the theatre...**(play)

공연장...

(GⓄNG-YⓤⓗN-JⓐⓗNG)

Is it okay to invite you to go to...?

당신을 ~에 초대해도 될까요?

DⓐⓗNG-SHⓘN-ⓞⓤL (KⓄN-SSⓤⓗ-Tⓞⓤ) ~ ⓔ
CHⓄ-Dⓐ-Hⓐ-DⓄ DWⓔL-GGⓐⓗ-YⓄ

PHRASEMAKER

▶ **A health club**

헬스클럽(을)…

HĕL-Sⓞⓤ-Kⓞⓤ-LⓤⓑB…

▶ **A swimming pool…**

수영장(을)…

SⓞⓞL-YⓤⓑNG-JⓐⓑNG…

▶ **A tennis court…**

테니스장(을)…

Tĕ-NⒺⒺ-Sⓞⓤ-JⓐⓑNG…

▶ **A golf course…**

골프장(을)…

GⓞⓛL-Pⓞⓤ-JⓐⓑNG…

…where can I find?

~어디에서 찾을 수 있나요?

…ⓤⓑ-DⒺⒺ-ĕ-Sⓤⓑ CHⓐⓑ-JⓞⓤL
Sⓞⓞ ⒾN-Nⓐⓑ-Yⓞ

HEALTH

Hopefully you will not need medical attention on your trip. If you do, it is important to communicate basic information regarding your condition.

- Travelers to Korea are urged to obtain overseas medical insurance which includes hospitalization and medical evacuation.

- If you take prescription medicine, carry your prescription with you.

- Take a small first-aid kit with you. You may want to include basic cold, anti-diarrhea, and allergy medications. However, you should be able to find most items like aspirin locally.

- It is important to drink bottled water as well as using it for brushing your teeth.

- Hospitals and medical clinics are located in South Korea with pharmacies close by. General hospitals with international clinics offer English speaking doctors.

KEY WORDS

Ambulance

구급차

G⓪⓪-G⓪⓪P-CHⓐⓗ

Dentist

치과의사

CH㋓㋓-GGWⓐⓗ-⓪⓪㋓㋓-Sⓐⓗ

Doctor

의사

⓪⓪㋓㋓-Sⓐⓗ

Emergency

위급상황

W㋓㋓-G⓪⓪P-SⓐⓗNG-HWⓐⓗNG

Hospital

병원

BY⓾NG-W⓾N

Prescription

처방전

CH⓾-BⓐⓗNG-J⓾N

USEFUL PHRASES

I am sick.

저는 아파요.

J⒰-N⒪N ⓐh-Pⓐh-Y⓪

I need a doctor.

의사가 필요해요.

⒰⒠-Sⓐh-Gⓐh
P①-RY⓪-Hⓔ-Y⓪

It's an emergency!

위급 상황 이예요!

Wⓔ-G⒪P
Sⓐh-NG-HWⓐh-NG-ⓔ-Yⓔ-Y⓪

Call an ambulance!

구급차를 불러줘xx요!

G⓪⓪-G⒪P-CHⓐh-R⒪L
B⓪⓪L-L⒰-J⓪⓪-Sⓔ-Y⓪

I have a heart condition.

심장병이 있어요.

SH①M-Jⓐh-NG-BY⒰-NG-ⓔ
ⓔ-SS⒰-Y⓪

I'm allergic to...

~에 알레르기가 있어요.

...ⓔ ⓐhL-Lⓔ-Ⓡⓞⓤ-Gⓔⓔ-Gⓐh
ⓔⓔ-SSⓤh-Yⓞ

I'm pregnant.

임신중이예요.

ⓘM-SHⓘN-JⓞⓞNG-ⓔⓔ-Yⓔ-Yⓞ

I'm diabetic.

당뇨가 있어요.

DⓐhNG-NYⓞ-Gⓐh ⓔⓔ-SSⓤh-Yⓞ

I have high blood pressure.

저는 고혈압이예요.

Jⓤh-NⓞⓤN
Gⓞ-HYⓤh-ⓇⓐhP-ⓔⓔ-Yⓔ-Yⓞ

I have low blood pressure.

저는 저혈압이예요.

Jⓤh-NⓞⓤN
Jⓤh-HYⓤh-ⓇⓐhP-ⓔⓔ-Yⓔ-Yⓞ

PHRASEMAKER

Say what you need and then
go to the bottom of the page and
say ...Pⓘ-ⓇYⓄ-Hⓔ-YⓄ.

▶ **A doctor...**

의사(가)…

ⓄⓊⒺⒺ-Sⓐⓗ...

▶ **A dentist...**

치과의사(가)…

CHⒺⒺ-GGWⓐⓗ ⓄⓊⒺⒺ-Sⓐⓗ...

▶ **A nurse...**

간호사(가)…

GⓐⓗN-HⓄ-Sⓐⓗ-Kⓐⓗ...

▶ **An eye doctor...**

안과의사(가)…

ⓐⓗN-GGWⓐⓗ-ⓄⓊⒺⒺ-Sⓐⓗ...

▶ **A pharmacist...**

약사(가)…

Yⓐⓗ-SSⓐⓗ...

...I need

~필요해요.

...Pⓘ-ⓇYⓄ-Hⓔ-YⓄ

PHRASEMAKER
(AT THE PHARMACY)

▶ **Aspirin...**

아스피린(이)...

ⓐh-Sⓞⓤ-P①-Ⓡ①N...

▶ **Band-Aids...**

반창고(가)...

BⓐhN-CHⓐhNG-Gⓞ...

▶ **Cough medicine...**

기침약(이)...

GⒺⒺ-CH①M-YⓐhK...

▶ **Ear medicine...**

귀약(이)...

GWⒺⒺ-YⓐhK...

▶ **Eye medicine...**

눈약(이)...

NⓞⓞN-YⓐhK...

...do you have?

~있나요?

...①N-Nⓐh-Yⓞ

BUSINESS TRAVEL

It is important to show appreciation and interest in another person's language and culture, particularly when doing business. A few well-pronounced phrases can make a great impression.

- Business cards are essential. If possible, ensure that one side is printed in Korean and one side in English.

- Use both hands when accepting or offering a business card or gift.

- Take time to look at the card before putting it down.

- Waving you hands about or making loud noises is considered impolite.

- Don't write a Korean name in "red" ink.

- Business dress is conservative.

- It is important to give a firm hand shake both when greeting and leaving your Korean partners.

- Initially, meetings will begin with some small talk before moving on to business discussion. In most cases, older age among your Korean business counterparts reflects seniority.

KEY WORDS

Appointment (business)

예약 / 약속

Y@K-SS◎K / Yℯ Y@K

Business card

명함

MY◎NG-H@M

Meeting

회의 / 미팅

HWℯ-◎◎ℰ

Marketing

마케팅

M@-Kℯ-TℰℰNG

Office

사무실

S@-M◎◎-SH①L

Presentation

발표

B@L-PY◎

USEFUL PHRASES

I have an appointment with...

저는 ~하고 예약이 있어요...

J⑨-N⑳N (First and Last Name)

H⑨N-G⓪ Y⑨-Y⑨-G㊙

㊙-SS⑨-Y⓪

My name is...

제 이름은...입니다.

J⑨ ㊙-R⑳-M⑳N (First and Last Name)

⓪M-N㊙-D⑨

Pleased to meet you.

만나서 반가워요.

M⑨N-N⑨-S⑨

B⑨N-G⑨-W⑨-Y⓪

Here is my card.

제 명함이에요.

J⑨ MY⑨NG-H⑨M-㊙-Y⑨-Y⓪

I need an interpreter.

통역사가 필요해요.

T⓪NG-Y⑨K-S⑨-G⑨

P⓪-RY⓪-H⑨-Y⓪

Please write your address.

주소를 써 주세요.

J⊚⊚-SO-ᖇ⊚uL SSuh J⊚⊚-Sĕ-YO

Please write your phone number.

전화번호를 써 주세요.

JuhN-HW⊕h-Puh N-HO-ᖇ⊚uL
SSuh J⊚⊚-Sĕ-YO

This is my phone number.

제 전화 번호예요.

JuhN-HW⊕h-BuhN-HO-Yĕ-YO

His name is...

그의 이름은...이예요.

G⊚u-⊚uEE EE-ᖇ⊚u-M⊚uN(Name)EE-Yĕ-YO

Her name is...

그녀의 이름은...이예요.

K⊚u-NYuh-⊚uEE EE-ᖇ⊚u-M⊚uN(Name)EE-Yĕ-YO

Good-bye (Said to the person staying as you leave.)

안녕히 계세요.

⊕h-NYuhNG-HEE Gĕ-Sĕ-YO

Good-bye (Said to the person leaving.)

안녕히 가세요.

⊕h-NY⊚NG-HEE G⊕h-Sĕ-YO

PHRASEMAKER

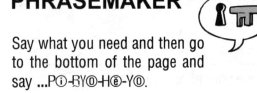

Say what you need and then go to the bottom of the page and say ...P①-BY⑩-H⑥-Y⑩.

▶ **A computer...**

컴퓨터(가)...

K⑩M-PY⑩-T⑩...

▶ **A copy machine...**

복사 기계(가) ...

B⑩K-S⑨ⓗ   G㋓-G⑥...

▶ **A conference room...**

회의실(이)...

HW⑥-⑩㋓-SH①L...

▶ **A fax machine...**

팩스 기계...

P⑧K-S⑩   G㋓-⑥...

▶ **An interpreter...**

통역사(가)...

T⑩NG-Y⑩K-S⑨ⓗ...

▶ **A lawyer...**

변호사(가)...

BYⓤN-HⓄ-Sⓐ...

▶ **A notary...**

계약서(가)...

Gⓔ-Yⓐ K-Sⓤ...

▶ **A pen...**

펜(이)...

Pⓔ N...

▶ **Stamps...**

우표(가)...

ⓞⓞ-PYⓄ...

▶ **Typing paper...**

종이(가)...

JⓄNG-ⓔ ...

...I need

~필요해요.

...P①-BYⓄ-Hⓔ-YⓄ

GENERAL INFORMATION

Korea enjoys climate conditions much like North America, with four seasons: spring, summer, autumn, and winter.

SEASONS

Spring

봄

BOM

Summer

여름

Yuh-ROum

Autumn

가을

Gah-ouL

Winter

겨울

KYuh-ooL

THE DAYS

Monday

월요일

WⓤhL-RYⓄ-ⓘL

Tuesday

화요일

HWⓐh-YⓄ-ⓘL

Wednesday

수요일

Sⓞⓞ-YⓄ-ⓘL

Thursday

목요일

MⓄ-GYⓄ-ⓘL

Friday

금요일

GⓞⓤM-YⓄ-ⓘL

Saturday

토요일

TⓄ-YⓄ-ⓘL

Sunday

일요일

ⓘ-RYⓄ-ⓘL

THE MONTHS

January	**February**
일월	이월
ⓘ-RⓤⓗL	ⒺⒺ-WⓤⓗL
March	**April**
삼월	사월
SⓐⓗM-WⓤⓗL	Sⓐⓗ-WⓤⓗL
May	**June**
오월	육월
ⓄO-WⓤⓗL	Yⓞⓞ-GWⓤⓗL
July	**August**
칠월	팔월
CHⓘ-RⓤⓗL	Pⓐⓗ-RⓤⓗL
September	**October**
구월	십월
Gⓞⓞ-WⓤⓗL	SⓘP-WⓤⓗL
November	**December**
십일월	십이월
SHⓘ-Bⓘ-RⓤⓗL	SHⓘ-BⒺⒺ-WⓤⓗL

COLORS

Black	**White**
검정색	하얀색
KⓤM-JⓤNG-SⓐK	Hⓐh-YⓐhN-SⓐK
Blue	**Brown**
파랑색	갈색
Pⓐh-RⓐhNG-SⓐK	KⓐhL-SⓐK
Gray	**Gold**
회색	금색
HWⓔⓔ-SⓐK	KⓞⓤM-SⓐK
Orange	**Yellow**
주황색	노랑색
Jⓞⓞ-HWⓐhNG-SⓐK	Nⓞ-RⓐhNG-SⓐK
Red	**Green**
빨강색	초록색
BBⓐhL-GⓐhNG-SⓐK	CHⓞ-RⓞK-SⓐK
Pink	**Purple**
분홍색	보라색
BⓞⓞN-HⓞNG-SⓐK	Pⓞ-Rⓐh-SⓐK

NUMBERS

0 영 / 공 Y⑩NG / G⑩NG	**1** 일 ㋐L	**2** 이 ㋐
3 삼 S⑳M	**4** 사 S⑳	**5** 오 ⑩	**6** 육 Y⑳K

3 삼 S⑳M	**4** 사 S⑳	**5** 오 ⑩	**6** 육 Y⑳K
7 칠 CH㋺L	**8** 팔 P⑳L	**9** 구 G⑳	**10** 십 SH㋺P

11 십일 SH㋺-B㋺L	**12** 십이 SH㋺-B㋐
13 십삼 SH㋺P-SS⑳M	**14** 십사 SH㋺P-S⑳
15 십오 SH㋺P-⑩	**16** 십육 SH㋺P-Y⑳K
17 십칠 SH㋺P-CH㋺L	**18** 십팔 SH㋺P-P⑳L

19	**20**
십구	이십
SHⓘP-Gⓞⓞ	ⒺⒺ-SHⓘP
30	**40**
삼십	사십
SⓐⓗM-SHⓘP	Sⓐⓗ-SHⓘP
50	**60**
오십	육십
Ⓞ-SHⓘP	YⓞⓞK-SSHⓘP
70	**80**
칠십	팔십
CHⓘL-SSHⓘP	PⓐⓗL-SSHⓘP
90	**100**
구십	백
Kⓞⓞ-SHⓘP	BⓐⓗK
1,000	**1,000,000**
천	백만
CHⓤⓗN	BⓐⓗNG-MⓐⓗN

DICTIONARY

Each English entry is followed by the Korean word in the Hangul script followed by the EPLS Vowel Symbol System. Masculine and feminine nouns are not defined as they are not a part of Korean language. Words followed by (I) or (to) indicate a verb.

A

a lot 많이 M@h-N€€

a little 조금 JO-K◎M

accident 사고 S@h-GO

accommodation (lodging) 설비 / 시설 S◎K-SS◎

address 주소 J◎◎-SO

admission 입학 €€P-H@hK

afraid (to be) 두려워 D◎◎-BY@h-W@h-H@h-D@h

after 나중에 N@h-J◎◎NG-€

afternoon 오후 O-H◎◎

air-conditioning 에어컨 €-@h-KON

aircraft 항공기 H@hNG-GONG-G€€

airline 항공 H@hNG-GONG

airport 공항 GONG-H@hNG

aisle 통로 TONG-BO

all 모두 MO-Doo

almost 거의 Guh-EE

alone 혼자 HON-Jah

also 또한 DDO-HahN

always 항상 HahNG-SahNG

ambulance 구급차 Koo-GooP-CHah

American 미국인 MEE-Goo-GiN

and 그리고 Kou-BEE-GO

another 또 다른한개 DDO-Dah-BouN-HahN-Gah

anything 아무거나 ah-Moo-Guh-Nah

apartment 아파트 ah-Pah-Tou

appetizers 에피타이저 e-PEE-Tah-EE-Juh

apple 사과 Sah-GWah

appointment 약속 YahK-SSOK

April 사월 Sah-WuhL

arrival 도착 DO-CHahK

ashtray 재떨이 Ja-DDuh-BEE

aspirin 아스피린 ah-Sou-Pi-BiN

attention 주의 Joo-EE

August 팔월 Pah-BuhL

Australia 호주 HO-Joo

Australian 호주 사람 HO-Joo-EE-Sah-BahM

author 저자   J@h-J@h

automobile 자동차   J@h-D©NG-CH@h

autumn (season) 가을   G@h-⨀⨀L

avenue 가로   G@h-R©L

awful 지독한   J㋙-D©K-H@h-D@h

B

baby 아기   @h-G㋙

babysitter 어린애 봐주는 사람
   @h-R①-N㋙ P@h-J⨀⨀-N⨀⨀N-S@h-R@hM

bacon 베이컨   B㋙-㋙-K@hN

bad 나쁘다   N@h-BB⨀⨀-D@h

bag 가방   G@h-B@hNG

baggage 수화물   S⨀⨀-HW@h-M⨀⨀L

bake 굽다   G⨀⨀P-D@h

bakery 빵집   PP@hNG-J①P

banana 바나나   B@h-N@h-N@h

Band-Aid 반창고   B@hN-CH@hNG-G©

bank 은행   ⨀⨀N-H@hNG

barbershop / beauty salon 이발소/미용실
   ㋙-B@hL-S© / M㋙-Y©NG-SH①L

bartender 바텐더   B@h-T㋙N-D@h

bath 목욕   M©-GY©K

bathing suit 수영복 SOO-YꞸG-BOK

bathroom 욕실 YOK-SHOL

battery (small) 건전지 KꞸN-JꞸN-JEE

battery (car) 배터리 BBah-DDa-REE

beach 바닷가 Bah-DahT-GGah

beautiful (to be) 아름답다 ah-RꞸM-DahP-Dah

bed 침대 CHIM-Da

beef 쇠고기 SWE-GO-GEE

beer 맥주 Ma K-JOO

bellboy 벨보이 BOL-BO-EE

belt 벨트 BOL-TOO

big 크다 KOO-Dah

bill (meal or invoice) 계산서 KE-SahN-SꞸ

black (color) 검정색 KꞸM-JꞸNG-Sa K

blanket 담요 DahM-YO

blue (color) 파랑색 Pah-RahNG-Sa K

boat 배 Ba

book 책 CHa K

bookstore 책방 CHa K-BBahNG

border 국경 GOOK-GYꞸNG

boy 소년 SO-NYꞸN

bracelet 팔지 Pah L-JJEE

brakes 브레이크 BⓄⓊ-Rⓔ-EE-KⓄⓊ

bread 빵 PPⓐNG

breakfast 조반 JⓄ-BⓐN

brother 형제 HYⓤⓗNG-Jⓔ

brown (color) 갈색 GⓐL-Sⓐ̄K

building 건물 GⓤⓗN-MⓄⓄL

bus 버스 Bⓤⓗ-SⓄⓊ

bus station 버스 정거장
      Bⓤⓗ-SⓄⓊ JⓐNG-Gⓐ-JⓐNG

bus stop 버스 정류장
      Bⓤⓗ-SⓄⓊ JⓐNG-Gⓐ-JⓐNG

business 사업 Sⓐ-ⓤⓗP

butter 버터 Bⓤⓗ-Tⓤⓗ

buy (to) 사다 Sⓐ-DⒶ

C

cab 택시 Tⓐ̄K-SEE

call (to) 부르다 BⓄⓄ-RⓄⓊ-Dⓐ

camera 사진기 Sⓐ-Jⓘ̄N-GEE

Canada 캐나다 Kⓐ̄-Nⓐ-Dⓐ

Canadian 캐나다 사람
      Kⓐ̄-Nⓐ-Dⓐ̄-Sⓐ-BⓐM

candy 사탕 Sⓐ-TⓐNG

car 자동차 Jⓐ-DⓄNG-CHⓐ

carrot 당근 D@NG-G@N

castle 성곽 S@NG-GW@K

celebration 축하 CH@K-H@

center (place, position) 센터 S@N-T@

cereal (cold) 씨리얼 ㄴ S@-R@-@L

chair 의자 @@-J@

champagne 샴페인 SH@M-P@-@N

change (to) 바꾸다 B@-GG@-D@

change (money) 환전하다 HW@N-J@N-H@-D@

cheap 싸요 SS@-Y@

check (bill) 계산서 G@-S@N-S@

cheers! 환호! HW@N-H@

cheese 치즈 CH@-J@

chicken 닭 D@LK

child 아이 @-@

chocolate 초콜렛 CH@-K@L-L@T

church 교회 KY@-HW@

cigar 씨가 SS@-G@

cigarette 담배 D@M-B@

city 도시 D@-SH@

clean 깨끗하다 GG@-GG@T-H@-D@

close (proximity, intimacy) 가깝다 G@-GG@P-D@

closed 닫히다 DⓐT-CHⒺⒺ-Dⓐ

clothes 옷 ⓄT

cocktail 칵테일 KⓐK-TⒺ-ⓘL

coffee 커피 Kⓤⓗ-PⒺⒺ

cold (to be) 춥다 CHⓄⓄP-Dⓐ

comb 빗 BⓘT

company 회사 HWⒺ-Sⓐ

computer 컴퓨터 KⓤⓗM-PYⓄⓄ-Tⓤⓗ

concert 연주회 YⓤⓗN-JⓄⓄ-HWⒺ

conference 회의 HWⒺ-ⓞⓤⒺⒺ

congratulations 축하해요 CHⓄⓄK-Kⓐ-HⒺ-YO

copy machine 복사기계 BⓄK-Sⓐ-GⒺⒺ-GⒺ

corn 옥수수 ⓄK-SⓄⓄ-SⓄⓄ

cough medicine 기침약 GⒺⒺ-CHⓘM-YⓐK

crab 게 GⒺ

cream 크림 KⓄⓤ-BⒺⒺM

credit card 크래딧 카드 KⓄⓤ-Bⓐ-DⓘT Kⓐⓗ-DⓄⓤ

cup 컵 KⓤⓗP

customs 세관 SⒺ-GWⓐN

D

dance (to) 춤추다 CHⓄⓄM-CHⓄⓄ-Dⓐ

dangerous 위험한 WⒺⒺ-HⓤⓗM-Hⓐ N

date (calendar) 날짜 NAL-JJah

day 일 iL

December 십이월 SHiP-EE-WuhL

delicious 맛있는 MahT-SHi-Min

delighted 기쁘다 GEE-Boo-Dah

dentist 치과의사 CHEE-GGWah-ooEE-Sah

deodorant 디오드런트 DEE-O-Doo-RuhN-Too

department store 백화점 BaK-HWah-JuhM

departure 출발 CHool-BahL

dessert 디저트/후식 DEE-JuhT-oo / Hoo-SHiK

detour 우회 oo-HWē

diabetes 당뇨병 DahNG-NYO-BYuhNG

diarrhea 설사 SuhL-Sah

dictionary 사전 Sah-JuhN

dinner 저녁 Juh-NYuhK

direction 방향 BahNG-HYahNG

dirty 더럽다 Duh-RuhP-Dah

disabled person 장애인(자) JahNG-ā-iN

discount 할인 Hah-RiN

distance 거리 Kuh-REE

doctor 의사 ooEE-Sah

documents 서류 Suh-RYoo

dollar 달러 DⓐL-Lⓤⓗ

down 아래로 ⓐh-Rⓐ-Rⓞ

downtown 도심지 Dⓞ-SH①M-Jⓔⓔ

drink (beverage) 음료 ⓞⓤM-RYⓞ

drugstore 약방 YⓐK-PPⓐNG

dry cleaner 세탁소 Sⓔ-TⓐⓗK-Sⓞ

duck (animal) 오리 ⓞ-Rⓔⓔ

E

ear 귀 KWⓔⓔ

earache 귀통증 GWⓔⓔ-TⓞNG-JJⓐNG

early 일찍 ①L-JJ①K

east 동쪽 DⓞNG-JJⓞK

easy 쉬운 SH①P-DDⓐⓗ

eat (to) 먹다 MⓤⓗK-Dⓐⓗ

egg 계란 Gⓔ-RⓐⓗN

electricity 전기 JⓤN-Gⓔⓔ

elevator 엘리베이터 ⓔL-Lⓔⓔ-Bⓔ-Tⓤⓗ

embassy 대사관 Dⓐ-Sⓐⓗ-GWⓐⓗN

emergency 위급상황
    Wⓔⓔ-GⓞⓤP-SⓐⓗNG-HWⓐⓗNG

England 영국 YⓤⓗNG-GⓞⓞK

English 영어 YⓤⓗNG-ⓤⓗ

enough! 충분해요! CHⓞNG-BⓞN-Hⓐ-Yⓞ

entrance 입구 ⒺP-GGⓞ

envelope 봉투 BⓞNG-Tⓞ

evening 저녁 Jⓤ-NYⓤK

everything 모두 / 전부 MⓄ-Dⓞ / JⓤN-Bⓞ

excellent 우수하다 ⓞ-Sⓞ-Hⓐ-Dⓐ

excuse me! 실례합니다 SHⓘ-Lⓔ-HⓐM-NⒺ-Dⓐ

exit 출구 CHⓞL-Gⓞ

expensive 비싸다 BⒺ-SSⓐ-Dⓐ

eye 눈 NⓞN

eye medicine 눈약 NⓞN-YⓐK

F

face 얼굴 ⓤL-GⓞL

far 멀다 MⓤL-Dⓐ

fare (charge) 운임 ⓞN-ⓘM

fast 빠른 BBⓐ-Bⓞ-Dⓐ

father 아버지 ⓐ-Bⓤ-JⒺ

fax (document) 팩스 PⓐK-Sⓞ

fax machine 팩스 기계 PⓐK-Sⓞ GⒺ-Gⓔ

February 이월 Ⓔ-WⓤL

few 적다 JⓤK-Dⓐ

film (movie) 영화 YⓤNG-HWⓐ

film (camera) 필름 PⓘL-LⓞM

finger 손가락 SⓞN-GGⓐh-Bⓐh)K

fire extinguisher 소화기 SO-HWⓐh-GⒺ

fire! (emergency) 불이야 Bⓞⓞ-RⒺⒺ-Yⓐh

first (original) 첫째 CHⓤhT-JJⒺ

fish 생선 SⓐNG-SⓤhN

flight 비행 BⒺⒺ-HⓐNG

florist shop 꽃가게 GⓞT-Gⓐh-GⒺ

flower 꽃 GGⓞT

food 음식 ⓞⓤM-SHⓘK

foot 발 Bⓐh)L

fork 포크 POⒹ-Kⓞⓤ

fresh 신선한 SHⓘN-SⓤhN-Hⓐh)N

Friday 금요일 GⓞⓤM-YOⒹ-ⓘL

fried 튀긴 TⒺⒺ-GⓘN Gⓐh)

friend 친구 CHⓘN-Gⓞⓞ

fruit 과일 GWⓐh)-ⓘL

funny 재미있는 JⒺ-MⒺⒺ-ⓘN-Nⓞⓤ)N

G

gas station 주유소 Jⓞⓞ-Yⓞⓞ-SO

gasoline 가솔린 Kⓐh)-SⓞL-LⒺⒺN

gate 문 Mⓞⓞ)N

gift 선물 SⓐN-MⓄL

girl 여자 Yⓤh-Jⓐh

glass (drinking) 유리잔 YⓄⓄ-RⒺⒺ-Jⓐh

glasses (eye) 안경 ⓐN-GYⓤhNG

gloves 장갑 JⓐhNG-Gⓐh P

go (to) 가다 Gⓐh-Dⓐh

gold (color) 금색 GⓄⓄM-Sⓐ̂K

golf 골프 GⓄL-PⓄu

golf course 골프장 GⓄL-PⓄu-Jⓐh NG

good 좋다 CHⓄT-Dⓐh

good bye 안녕히가세요 (said to the person leaving)
ⓐN-NYⓤhNG-HⒺⒺ Gⓐh-SⒺ-YO

good bye 안녕히계세요 (said to the person staying)
ⓐN-NYⓤhNG-HⒺⒺ GⒺ-SⒺ-YO

goose 거위 Gⓤh-WⒺⒺ

grape 포도 PⓄ-DⓄ

grateful 고맙게 여기는
GO-Mⓐh P-GⒺ Yⓤh-GⒺⒺ-NⓄN

gray (color) 회색 HWⒺ-Sⓐ̂K

green (color) 초록색 CHⓄ-RⓄK-Sⓐ̂K

grocery store 식품점 SHⒾK-PⓄⓄM-Jⓐh M

group 그룹 GⓄu-RⓄⓄP

guide 가이드 G(ah)-(EE)-D(ow)

H

hair 머리카락, 털 M(uh)-R(EE)-K(ah)-R(ah) / T(uh)L

hairbrush 머리빗 M(uh)-R(EE)-B(i)T

haircut 이발 (EE)-B(ah)L

ham 햄 H(a)M

hamburger 햄버거 H(a)M-B(uh)-G(uh)

hand 손 S(O)N

happy 기쁘다 G(EE)-BB(ow)-D(ah)

have (to) 가지다 G(ah)-J(EE)-D(ah)

he 그는 G(ow)-N(ow)N

head 머리 M(uh)-R(EE)

headache 두통 D(oo)-T(O)NG

health club (gym) 헬스 클럽 H(e)L-S(ow)-K(O)L-L(uh)B

heart disease 심장병 SH(i)M-J(ah)NG-BY(uh)NG

heart 심장 SH(i)M-J(ah)NG

heat 열 Y(uh)L

hello 안녕하세요 (ah)N-NY(uh)NG-H(ah)-S(e)-Y(O)

help! (emergency) 도와주세요 D(O)-W(ah)-J(oo)-S(e)-Y(O)

holiday 휴일 HY(oo)-(i)L

hospital 병원 BY(uh)NG-W(uh)N

hotel 호텔 H(O)-T(e)L

hour 시간 SHEE-GahN

how 어떻게요 uh-DDuh-Kê

hurry up! 서둘러 주세요 Suh-DooL-Luh-Joo-Sê-YO

husband 남편 NahM-PYuhN

I

I 저 / 나 Juh / Nah

ice 얼음 uh-Boom

ice cream 아이스크림 ah-EE-Soo-Koo-REEM

ill 아프다 ah-Poo-Dah

important 중요한 JOONG-YO-Hahn

indigestion 소화 불량 SO-HWah-BooL-LYahNG

information 정보 CHuhNG-BO

information (directory assistance 114) 정보 OL-OL-SSah

interpreter 통역사 TONG-YuhK-Sah

J

jacket 자켓 Jah-KêT

jam 잼 JâM

January 일월 O-BuhL

jewelry 보석 BO-SuhK

jewelry store 보석상 BO-SuhK-SahNG

job   일   ⓘL

juice   주스   Jⓞⓞ-Sⓞⓤ

July   칠월   CHⓘ-BⓤⓗL

June   육월   Yⓞⓞ-GWⓤⓗL

K

ketchup   케첩   Kⓔ-CHⓤⓗP

key   열쇠   YⓤⓗL-SWⓔ

kiss   키스   Kⓘ-Sⓞⓤ

knife   칼   KⓐⓗL

know (need to know something)   알아야한다
    ⓐⓗ-Rⓐⓗ-Yⓐⓗ-Hⓐⓗ-Dⓐⓗ

L

ladies room   여자 화장실
    Yⓤⓗ-Jⓐⓗ   HWⓐⓗ-JⓐⓗNG-SHⓘL

lady   숙녀   SⓞⓞNG-Yⓤⓗ

lamb   양   YⓐⓗNG-Gⓘ-Gⓔⓔ

language   언어   ⓤⓗN-ⓤⓗ

large   큰   KⓞⓤN

late (to be)   늦다   NⓞⓤT-Dⓐⓗ

laundry   세탁   Sⓔ-TⓐⓗK-MⓞⓞL

lawyer   변호사   BYⓤⓗN-Hⓘ-Sⓐⓗ

left (direction)   왼쪽   WⓔN-JJⓞK

leg 다리 Dah-REE

lemon 레몬 LE-MON

less 적다 JuhK-Dah

letter 편지 PYuhN-JEE

lettuce 상치 Sah NG-CHEE

light 빛 BiT

like 좋아하다 JO-ah-Hah-Dah

lips 입술 EEP-SooL

lipstick 립스틱 LiP-Soo-TiK

little (amount/size) 적다 JuhK-Dah

live (to) 살다 Sah L-Dah

lobster 바닷가재 Bah-Dah T-Gah-Jä

long 긴 GEEN

lost 분실한 BooN-SHiL-Hah N

love 사랑 Sah-Rah NG

luck 운 ooN

luggage 짐 JiM

lunch 점심 JuhM SHiM

M

maid 도우미 DO-oo-MEE

mail 우편 oo-PYuhN

makeup 메이크업 / 화장
   MⒺ-EE-KⓄⓄ-uhP / HWⓐh-JⓐhNG

man 남자 NⓐhM-Jⓐh

map 지도 JEE-DⓄ

March 삼월 Sⓐh-MuhL

market (retail) 시장 SHEE-JⓐhNG

matches 성냥 SuhNG-NYⓐhNG

May 오월 Ⓞ-WuhL

mayonnaise 마요네즈 Mⓐh-YⓄ-NⒺ-JⓄⓄ

meal 식사 SHⒾK-Sⓐh

meat 고기 GⓄ-GEE

mechanic 기계공 GEE-GⒺ-GⓄNG

meeting 회의 HWⒾ-EE

mens' restroom 남자화장실
   NⓐhM-Jⓐh-HWⓐh-JⓐhNG-SHⒾL

menu 메뉴 MⒺ-NYⓄⓄ

message 메시지 MⒺ-SSⒺ-JEE

milk 우유 ⓄⓄ-YⓄⓄ

mineral water 미네랄 워터
   MEE-NⒺ-RⓐhL Wuh-Tuh

minute 분 BⓄⓄN

Miss 아가씨 ⓐh-Gⓐh-SSEE

mistake 실수 SHⒾL-SⓄⓄ

misunderstanding 오해 ⓞ-Hⓐ

moment 순간 SⓞⓞN-Gⓐⓝ

Monday 월요일 WⓤⓗL-BYⓞ-ⓘL

money 돈 DⓞN

month 달 / 월 DⓐⓗL / WⓤⓗL

monument 기념물 Gⓔⓔ-NYⓤⓗM-MⓞⓞL

more 더 Dⓤⓗ

morning 아침 ⓐⓗ-CHⓘM

mother 어머니 ⓤⓗ-Mⓤⓗ-Nⓔⓔ

mountain 산 SⓐⓝN

movie 영화 YⓤⓗNG-HWⓐⓗ

museum 박물관 BⓐⓝNG-MⓞⓞL-GWⓐⓝN

mushroom 버섯 Bⓤⓗ-SⓤⓗT

music 음악 ⓞⓤ-MⓐⓗK

mustard 겨자 GYⓤⓗ-Jⓤⓗ

N

nail polish 메니큐어 Mⓔ-Wⓔⓔ-KYⓞⓞ-ⓤⓗ

name 이름 ⓔⓔ-BⓤⓤM

napkin 냅킨 NⓐⓐP-KⓘN

near 가깝다 Gⓐⓗ-GGⓐⓗP-Dⓐⓗ

neck 목 MⓞK

need (l) ～필요 ...PⓘL-BYⓞ-Hⓔ-Yⓞ

never 결코 GY⑩L-K⑩

newspaper 신문 SH①N-M⑩N

night 밤 B⑩M

nightclub 나이트클럽 N⑩-⑻-T⑩-K⑩L-L⑩B

no 아니요 ⑩-N⑻-Y⑩

no smoking 금연 G⑩M-Y⑩N

noon 정오 J⑩NG-⑩

north 북쪽 B⑩K-JJ⑩K

notary 공증인 G⑩NG-J⑩N-①N

November 십일월 SH①-B①-B⑩L

now 지금 J⑻-G⑩M

number 숫자 S⑩T-JJ⑩

nurse 간호사 G⑩N-H①-S⑩

O

occupied (bathroom / room) 차있다 / 들어가있다
   CH⑩-⑻T-D⑩ / D⑩-B⑩-G⑩-⑻T-D⑩

ocean 바다 B⑩-D⑩

October 십월 SH①-B⑩L

officer (police) 경찰관 KY⑩NG-CH⑩L-GW⑩N

oil 기름 G⑻-R⑩M

omelet 오믈렛 ⑩-M⑩-LL⑩T

one-way (road) 일방통행로
　　ⓘL-Bⓐh NG-TⓄNG-Hⓐh NG-Rⓞ

onion 양파 Yⓐh NG-Pⓐh

open (to) 열다 Yⓤh L-Dⓐh

opera 오페라 ⓞ-Pⓔ-Rⓐh

operator (telephone) 전화교환수
　　Jⓤh N-HWⓐh-KYⓄ-HWⓐh N-Sⓞⓞ

orange (color) 주황색 Jⓞⓞ-HWⓐh NG-SⓐⓔK

owner 소유자 SⓄ-Yⓞⓞ-Jⓐh

oyster 굴 Gⓞⓞ

P

package 포장 PⓄ-Jⓐh NG

pay 급여 Gⓞⓤ-BYⓤh

pain 고통 Gⓞ-TⓄNG

painting 그리다 Kⓞⓞ-Rⓔⓔ-Dⓐh

paper 종이 JⓄNG-ⓔⓔ

parking 주차 Jⓞⓞ-CHⓐh

partner (business) 동업자 DⓄNG-ⓤh P-Jⓐh

party (celebration) 잔치 Jⓐh N-CHⓔⓔ

passenger 여객 Yⓤh-GⓐⓔK

passport 여권 Yⓤh-GWⓤh N

pasta 파스타 Pⓐh-Sⓞⓤ-Tⓐh

pastry 패이스트리   Pⓐ-ⓔⓔ-Sⓞⓤ-Tⓞⓤ-Rⓔⓔ

pen 펜   PⓔN

pencil 연필   YⓤⓗN-PⓘL

pepper (black) 후추   Hⓞⓞ-CHⓞⓞ

perfume 향수   HYⓐⓗNG-Sⓞⓞ

person 사람   Sⓐⓗ-RⓐⓗM

pharmacist 약사   YⓐⓗK-SSⓐⓗ

pharmacy 약국   YⓐⓗK-GⓞⓞK

phone book 전화번호부   JⓤⓗN-HWⓐⓗ-PⓤⓗN-Hⓘ-Bⓞⓞ

photo 사진   Sⓐⓗ-JⓘN

photographer 사진사   Sⓐⓗ-JⓘN-Sⓐⓗ

pillow 베개   Bⓔ-Gⓐ

pink (color) 분홍색   BⓞⓞN-HⓞNG-SⓐK

pizza 피자   Pⓔⓔ-JJⓐⓗ

plastic 플라스틱   PⓞⓤL-ⓐⓗ-Sⓞⓤ-TⓘK

plate 접시   JⓤⓗP-SSHⓔⓔ

please 부탁드립니다
        Bⓞⓞ-TⓐⓗK-Dⓞⓤ-RⓘM-Nⓔⓔ-Dⓐⓗ

pleasure 기쁨   Gⓔⓔ-PPⓞⓤM

police 경찰   GYⓤⓗNG-CHⓐⓗL

police station 경찰서   GYⓤⓗNG-CHⓐⓗL-Sⓤⓗ

pork 돼지고기   TWⓔ-Jⓔⓔ-Gⓘ-Gⓔⓔ

porter 짐을 옮길사람
JI-MOL OLM-GOL-Sah-Bahm

post office 우체국 OO-CHE-GOOK

postcard 엽서 Yuhp-Suh

potato 감자 Gahm-Jah

pregnant (to be) 임신 IM-SHIN-Hah-Dah

prescription (medical) 처방전 CHuh-Bahng-Juhn

price 가격 Kah-GYuhK

problem 문제 MooN-Je

public 공공의 GONG-GONG-ouEE

public telephone 공중전화
GONG-JooNG-JuhN-HWah

purple (color) 보라색 BO-Rah-Sak

purse 지갑 JEE-GahP

Q

quality 질 JIL

question 질문 JIL-MooN

quickly 빨리 BBah-L-LEE

quit (to) 그만두다 Gou-Mahn-Doo-Dah

quiet! 조용히 하세요
JO-YONG-HEE Hah-Se-YO

R

radio 라디오 Rah-DEE-O

railroad 기찻길 GEE-CHah T-GiL

rain 비 BEE

raincoat 비옷 BEE-OT

razor blades 면도기 MYuhN-DO-GEE

ready (to be) 준비되다 JOON-BEE-DWE-Dah

receipt 영수증 YuhNG-SOO-JuhNG

recommend (to) 추천하다 CHOO-CHuhN-Hah-Dah

red (color) 빨강색 PPahL-GahNG-SaK

repeat 반복하다 BahN-BOK-Hah-Dah

reservation 예약 YE-YahK

restaurant 식당 SHiK-DDahNG

return (to) 돌아오다 DO-Rah-O-Dah

rice (cooked) 밥 PahP

rich 부자 POO-Jah

right (correct) 맞다 MahT-DDah

right (direction) 오른쪽 O-RuhN-JO

road 길 GiL

room 방 PahNG

round trip 왕복 WahNG-BOK

S

safe (hotel) 금고 K◍M-G◍

salad 샐러드 SⓐL-Lⓤ-D◍◍

sale 세일 / 할인 SSⒺ-ⓘL / Hⓐ-RⓘN

salmon 연어 Yⓤ-Nⓤ

salt 소금 S◍-G◍◍M

sandwich 샌드위치 SⓐN-D◍◍-WⒺ-CHⒺ

Saturday 토요일 T◍-Y◍-ⓘL

scissors 가위 Gⓐ-WⒺ

sculpture 조각 CH◍◍-Gⓐ⃝K

seafood 해산물 Hⓐ-Sⓐ⃝N-M◍◍L

season 계절 GⒺ-Jⓤ⃝L

seat 좌석 JWⓐ-Sⓤ⃝K

secretary 비서 BⒺⒺ-Sⓤ⃝

section 부분 B◍◍-B◍◍N

September 구월 G◍◍-Wⓤ⃝L

service 서비스 Sⓤ-BⒺⒺ-S◍◍

several 여러가지 Yⓤ-Rⓤ-Gⓐ-JⒺⒺ

shampoo 샴푸 SHⓐM-P◍◍

sheet (bed) 시트 SHⒺⒺ-T◍◍

shirt 셔츠 SHⓐ-SS◍◍

shoes 구두 G◍◍-D◍◍

shoe store 구두가게 GOO-DOO-GAH-Gē

shopping center 쇼핑센터 SHO-PĒNG SēN-Tuh

shower 샤워 SHah-Wuh

shrimp 새우 Sā-OO

sick 아프다 ah-POU-Dah

signature 싸인 Sah-īN

silence! 조용히 해주세요!
        JO-YONG-HĒE Hā-JOO-Sē-YO

single 하나의 Hah-Nah-ouĒE

sister (younger) 여동생 Yuh-DONG-Sāng

sister (older) 언니 uhN-NĒE

size 크기 Kou-GĒE

skin 피부 PĒE-BOO

skirt 치마 CHĒE-Mah

sleeve 소매 SO-Mā

slowly 천천히 CHuhN-CHuhN-HĒE

small (to be) (size) 작다 Jah K-Dah

smile (to) 미소짓다 MĒE-SO-JīT-Dah

smoke (to) 담배를 피우다
        Dah M-Bā-Boou PĒE-oo-Dah

soap 비누 BĒE-Noo

socks 양말 Yah NG-Mah L

some 조금 / 어떤 JO-GouM / uh-DDuhN

something 무언가 M∞-ah N-Gah

sometimes 때때로 DDã-Dã-RO

soon 곧 GOT

sorry (I am) 미안해요 MEE-ah N-HÊ-YO

soup 수프 S∞-Pou

south 남쪽 Nah M-JJOK

souvenir 기념품 GEE-NYuh M-P∞M

Spanish (language) 스페인어 Sou-PÊ-①N-uh

speed 속도 SOK-DO

spoon 숟가락 S∞T-Gah-Rah K

sport 운동 ∞N-DONG

spring (season) 봄 BOM

stairs 계단 GÊ-Dah N

stamp 우표 ∞-PYO

station 역 Yuh K

steak 스테이크 Sou-TÊ-EE-Kou

steamed 찐 JJ①M

stop! 멈춰주세요 MuhM-CHuh-J∞-SÊ-YO

store 가게 Gah-GÊ

storm 폭풍 POK-P∞NG

straight 똑바로 DDOK-Bah-RO

strawberry 딸기 DDah L-GGEE

street 길 GⓘL

string 줄 JⓞⓞL

subway 지하철 JⒺE-Hⓐ-CHⓤⓝL

sugar 설탕 SⓤⓝL-TⓐNG

suit (clothes) 정장 JⓤⓝNG-JⓐⓝNG

suitcase 여행 가방 Yⓤⓝ-HⓐNG Gⓐⓝ-BⓐⓝNG

summer 여름 Yⓤⓝ-RⓞⓤM

sun 해 / 태양 Hⓐ / Tⓐ-YⓐNG

suntan lotion 썬텐 로션 SSⓤⓝN-TⒺN LⓄ-SHⓤⓝN

Sunday 일요일 ⓘ-RYⓄ-ⓘL

sunglasses 선글라스 SⓤⓝN-ⓞⓞL-Lⓐⓝ-Sⓞⓤ

supermarket 슈퍼마켓 SYⓞⓞ-Pⓤⓝ-Mⓐⓝ-KⒺT

surprise 놀라다 NⓄL-Lⓐⓝ-Dⓐⓝ

sweet (to be) 달다 DⓐⓝL-Dⓐⓝ

swim (to) 수영하다 Sⓞⓞ-YⓤⓝNG-Hⓐⓝ-Dⓐⓝ

swimming pool 수영장 Sⓞⓞ-YⓤⓝNG-JⓐⓝNG

synagogue 회당 Yⓞⓞ-Tⓐ-ⓘN KYⓄ-HWⒺ

T

table 책상 TⒺ-EE-BⓞⓤL

tampon 생리대 SⓐNG-LⒺE-DⒺ

tape (sticky) 테이프 TⒺ-EE-Pⓞⓤ

tape recorder 카세트 / 녹음기
 KAH-SE-TOU NO-GOOM-GEE

tax 세금 SE-GOOM

taxi 택시 TAK-SEE

tea 차 CHAH

telephone 전화 CHOON-HWAH

television 티비 / 테렐비 TE-LE-BEE

temperature 온도 ON-DO

temple (worship) 절 JUH

tennis 테니스 TE-NEE-SOU

tennis court 테니스장 TE-NEE-SOU-JAHNG

thank you! 감사합니다 GAHM-SAH-HAHM-NEE-DAH

that 저것 JUH-GUHT

theater (movie) 영화관 YOONG-HWAH-GWAHN

there 저기 JUH-GEE

they 그들 GOU-DOOL

this 이것 EE-GUHT

thread 실 SHIL

throat 목 MOK

Thursday 목요일 MO-GYO-IL

ticket 표 PYO

tie (clothes) 넥타이 NEK-TAH-EE

time   시간   SHEE-Gah-N

tip (gratuity usually included)   팁   TOP

tire   타이어   Tah-EE-uh

toast (bread)   토스트   TO-Soo-Tou

tobacco   담배   Dah-M-Bã

today   오늘   O-Noo-L

toe   발가락   Bah-L-Gah-Rah-K

together   같이 / 함께   Gah-CHEE / Hah-M-GGê

toilet   화장실   HWah-Jah-NG-SHOL

toilet paper   화장지   HWah-Jah-NG-JEE

tomato   토마토   TO-Mah-TO

tomorrow   내일   Nã-OL

toothache   치통   CHEE-TONG

toothbrush   칫솔   CHEE-SOL

toothpaste   치약   CHEE-Yah-K

toothpick   이쑤시게   EE-Soo-SHEE-Gê

tour   관광   GWah-N-GWah-NG

tourist   관광객   GWah-N-GWah-NG-Kã-K

towel   수건   Soo-Guh-N

train   기차   GEE-CHah

travel agency   여행사   Yuh-Hã-NG-Sah

traveler's check 여행자 수표

　　YŰH-HÃNG-Jᵃ SÕO-PYÕ

trip 여행 YŰH-HÃNG

truth 진실 JĨN-SHĨL

Tuesday 화요일 HWᵃ-YÕ-ĨL

turkey 칠면조 CHĨL-MYŰN-JÕ

U

umbrella 우산 ÕO-Sᵃ N

understand (to) 이해하다 ẼE-HÃ-Hᵃ-Dᵃ

underwear 속옷 SÕ-GÕT

United Kingdom 영국 YᵃNG-GÕO

United States 미국 MẼE-GÕOK

university 대학교 Tẽ-Hᵃ-GGÕ

up 위 WẼE

urgent 위급하다 WẼE-GᵒOP-Hᵃ-Dᵃ

V

vacant 비어있다 BẼE-ᵘ-ẼET-DDᵃ

vacation 휴가 HYÕO-Gᵃ

valuable 가치 있는 Gᵃ-CHẼE-Gᵃ-ĨN-NᵒⁿN

vanilla 바닐라 Bᵃ-NĨL-Lᵃ

vegetables 야채 Yᵃ-CHÃ

view 관경 GWᵃN-GYŰNG

vinegar   식초   SHⓘK-CHⓄ

W

wait!   기다리세요   Gⓔⓔ-Dⓐⓗ-Rⓔⓔ-Sⓔ-YⓄ

waiter   웨이터   Wⓔ-ⓔⓔ-Tⓤⓗ

waitress   웨이트레스   ⓐⓗN-Nⓔⓔ

want (I)   원해요   WⓤⓗN-Hⓔ-YⓄ

wash (to)   씻다   SSⓘT-Dⓐⓗ

watch out!   조심하세요   JⓄ-SHⓘM-Hⓐⓗ-Sⓔ-YⓄ

water   물   MⓞⓞL

watermelon   수박   Sⓞⓞ-BⓐⓗK

we   우리   ⓞⓞ-Rⓔⓔ

weather   일기   ⓘL-GGⓔⓔ

Wednesday   수요일   Sⓞⓞ-YⓄ-ⓘL

week (this)   (이번)주   ⓔⓔ-BⓤⓗN-JJⓞⓞ

weekend   주말   Jⓞⓞ-MⓐⓗL

welcome   환영   HWⓐⓗN-YⓤⓗNG

well done (cooked in a steakhouse)   푹 익혀주세요
    PⓞⓞK-ⓔⓔ-KYⓤⓗ-Jⓞⓞ-Sⓔ-YⓄ

west   서쪽   Sⓤⓗ-JJⓄK

wheelchair   휠체어   HWⓔⓔL-CHⓔ-ⓤⓗ

when?   언제요?   ⓤⓗN-Jⓔ-YⓄ

where?   어디에서요?   ⓤⓗ-Dⓔⓔ-ⓔ-Sⓤⓗ-YⓄ

which? 어떤거요? ⓤN-DDⓤN-Gⓤh-Yⓞ

white 흰색 Hⓐh-YⓐhN-Sⓐ̄K

who? 누구요? Nⓞⓞ-Gⓞⓞ-Yⓞ

why? 왜요? Wⓐ̄-Yⓞ

wife 부인 Pⓞⓞ-ⓘN

wind 바람 Pⓐh-ⓇⓐhM

window 창 CHⓐhNG

wine 포도주 Pⓞ-Dⓞ-Jⓞⓞ

winter 겨울 KYⓤh-ⓞⓞL

with ～와 같이 Wⓐh Gⓐh-CHⓔⓔ

woman 여성 Yⓤh-SⓤhNG

wonderful 멋진 Mⓐh-JJⓘN

world 세계 Sⓔ̄-Gⓔ̄

wrong 틀리다 Tⓞ̄L-Lⓔⓔ-Dⓐh

XYZ

yellow (color) 노랑색 Nⓞ-ⓇⓐhNG-Sⓐ̄K

yes 네 Nⓔ̄ / Yⓔ̄

yesterday 어제 ⓤh-Jⓔ̄

you (polite or to an elder) 당신 DⓐhNG-SHⓘN

you (to a younger person or friend) 너 Nⓤh

zipper 지퍼 Jⓔⓔ-Pⓤh

zoo 동물원 DⓞNG-Mⓞⓞ-ⓇⓤhN

THANKS!

The nicest thing you can say to anyone in any language is "Thank you." Try some of these languages using the incredible Vowel Symbol System.

Spanish	French
GR(ah)́-S(EE)-(ah)S	M(ĕ)R-S(EE)́

German	Italian
D(ah)́N-K(uh)	GR(ah)́T-S(EE)-(ĕ)

Japanese	Chinese
D(O)́-M(O)	SH(EE)(ĕ) SH(EE)(ĕ)

Swedish

TⓐⓗK

Portuguese

Ⓞ-BR̃Ⓔ-Gⓐⓗ-DⓄ

Arabic

SHⓞⓞ-KRⓐⓗN

Greek

ěF-Hⓐⓗ-R̃Ⓔ-STⓞ́

Hebrew

Tⓞ-Dⓐⓗ́

Russian

SPⓐⓗ-SⒺ́-Bⓐⓗ

Swahili

ⓐⓗ-Sⓐⓗ́N-TⒶ

Dutch

DⓐⓗNK ⓞⓞ

Tagalog

Sⓐⓗ-Lⓐⓗ-Mⓐⓗ́T

Hawaiian

Mⓐⓗ-Hⓐⓗ́-LⓞLⓞ

INDEX

NOTES

QUICK REFERENCE PAGE

Hello

안녕하세요

ⓐN-NYⓤNG Hⓐ-Sⓔ-Yⓞ

Hello (Informal)

안녕

ⓐN-NYⓤNG

Yes   **No**   **Help!**

네   아니요   도와주세요

Nⓔ   ⓐ-NⒺ-Yⓞ   Dⓞ-Wⓐ-Jⓤ-Sⓔ-Yⓞ

Please

부탁드립니다

Bⓤ-TⓐK-Dⓞ-RⓘM-NⒺ-Dⓐ

Thank you

감사합니다

GⓐM-Sⓐ-HⓐM-NⒺ-Dⓐ

I'm sorry.

죄송합니다

CHⓔ-SONG-HⓐM-NⒺ-Dⓐ

I don't understand!

이해가 안되요

Ⓔ-Hⓐ-Gⓐ ⓐN-DWⓔ-Yⓞ